Charting the Course with Options Trading:

Demystifying the Risk, Mastering the Rewards - Your Comprehensive Roadmap to the World of Financial Derivatives

Gaston Chavez

Summary

Chapter 1: Introduction to Options Trading

In recent years, options trading has become an increasingly popular way for investors to manage their portfolios and generate income. Options are a powerful tool that can be used to manage risk, speculate on the future direction of a stock or index, and generate income from a portfolio. However, options trading can also be risky and complicated, and it is essential to have a solid understanding of the underlying mechanics before getting started.

This chapter will provide an introduction to options trading and will cover the basics of options contracts, including the differences between call and put options, the mechanics of options trading, and common strategies used by options traders.

Options Contracts

An option is a contract that gives the holder the right, but not the obligation, to buy or sell a financial asset at a specific price (the "strike price") on or before a specific date (the "expiration date"). The financial asset underlying an option can be a stock, an index, a commodity, or a currency.

There are two basic types of options contracts: call options and put options.

Call Options

A call option gives the holder the right, but not the obligation, to buy a financial asset at a specific price (the "strike price") on or before a specific date (the "expiration date"). If the stock price is higher than the strike price at expiration, the call option is "in the money" and the holder can buy the underlying asset at a discount to the market price. If the stock price is lower than the strike price at expiration, the call option is "out of the money" and expires worthless.

Put Options

A put option gives the holder the right, but not the obligation, to sell a financial asset at a specific price (the "strike price") on or before a specific date (the "expiration date"). If the stock price is lower than the strike price at expiration, the put option is "in the money" and the holder can sell the underlying asset at a premium to the market price. If the stock price is higher than the strike price at expiration, the put option is "out of the money" and expires worthless.

Mechanics of Options Trading

Options trading is conducted on options exchanges, which are similar to stock exchanges but specialize in options contracts. The two largest options exchanges in the United States are the Chicago Board Options Exchange (CBOE) and the International Securities Exchange (ISE).

To trade options, investors must open an options trading account with a brokerage firm that specializes in options trading (not all brokerage firms offer options trading). Once the account is open, investors can buy and sell options contracts through their broker's online trading platform or by calling their broker.

Options contracts have a number of key attributes that investors must be familiar with before trading:

• Underlying asset: The financial asset that the option gives the holder the right to buy or sell.

• Strike price: The price at which the option can be exercised.

• Expiration date: The date on which the option expires.

• Premium: The price that the holder pays for the option contract.

Options trading can be complicated due to the number of variables involved, including the intrinsic value of the option, the extrinsic value of the option, implied volatility, and time decay. To be successful at options trading, investors must have a solid understanding of these variables and the strategies that can be used to profit from them.

Options Trading Strategies

There are a wide variety of options trading strategies that investors can use to manage their portfolios and generate income. Here are some of the most common:

• Covered call: A covered call is a strategy in which the investor sells call options on a stock that they already own. This strategy is designed to generate income from the premium paid by the call option buyer, while also providing some downside protection in the event that the stock price declines.

• Protective put: A protective put is a strategy in which the investor buys a put option on a stock that they already own. This strategy is designed to provide downside protection in the event that the stock price declines.

• Long call: A long call is a strategy in which the investor buys a call option on a stock that they believe will increase in price. This strategy is designed to profit from an increase in the stock price without having to purchase the stock outright.

• Long put: A long put is a strategy in which the investor buys a put option on a stock that they believe will decrease in price. This strategy is designed to profit from a decrease in the stock price without having to sell the stock outright.

• Straddle: A straddle is a strategy in which the investor buys both a call option and a put option on the same stock, with the same strike price and expiration date. This strategy is designed to profit from a significant move in either direction.

• Strangle: A strangle is similar to a straddle, but the call and put options have different strike prices. This strategy is designed to profit from a significant move in either direction, but with less risk than a straddle.

Options trading can be a powerful tool for managing portfolio risk, generating income, and speculating on the future direction of a stock or index. However, options trading is also complex and can be risky. Before getting started with options trading, it is essential to have a solid understanding of the underlying mechanics and the strategies that can be used to profit from options contracts. With the right knowledge and strategy, options trading can be a valuable addition to any investor's toolkit.

Chapter 2: Understanding Call Options

Call options are one of the three most popular types of options used in the financial market. Options are contracts that give the holder the right, but not the obligation, to buy or sell an underlying asset at a specified price and time. Call options give the holder the right to buy an underlying asset at a specified price on or before a certain date. This chapter will cover the basics of call options, including how they work, why investors use them, and their advantages and disadvantages.

How Call Options Work

Let's start with an example. Suppose you believe that the price of a stock, XYZ, will increase over the next two months from its current price of $50 per share. You might consider buying a call option to profit from this anticipated price increase. A call option contract gives you the right to buy a certain number of shares of XYZ at a specified price, called the strike price, on or before a certain date, called the expiration date.

For example, you might buy a call option with a strike price of $55 and an expiration date two months from now. This means that you can buy 100 shares of XYZ for $55 per share at any time during the next two months. If the price of XYZ increases above $55 per share, you can exercise your option and buy the shares at the lower strike price of $55, even though the market price may be higher. You can then sell the shares on the open market at the higher market price and make a profit.

However, if the price of XYZ does not increase above $55 per share before the option expiration date, your option will expire worthless. You will lose the premium you paid to purchase the option, which is the price of the option contract. The premium is a fraction of the price of the underlying asset, typically between 1% and 10%.

Why Investors Use Call Options

There are many reasons why investors use call options. Some of the most common reasons include:

1. Speculation: Investors may use call options to speculate on the future price of an underlying asset. They may believe that the price will increase and make a profit by buying call options. Alternatively, they may believe that the price will decrease and choose to short the underlying asset by buying put options.

2. Hedging: Investors may use call options to hedge their existing investments. For example, if an investor owns a portfolio of stocks, they may buy call options on some of their holdings to protect against a potential downturn in the market.

3. Income: Investors who sell call options can generate income in the form of the option premium. This is a popular strategy used by professional traders who specialize in options trading.

4. Leverage: Buying call options allows investors to control a large amount of the underlying asset with a relatively small amount of capital. This can result in substantial returns if the trade is profitable, but also carries significant risk.

Advantages of Call Options

There are several advantages to using call options in your investment strategy:

1. Limited Risk: The most you can lose on a call option is the premium paid for the contract. This means you have a defined risk limit.

2. Unlimited Profit Potential: Call options offer unlimited profit potential, as there is no limit to how high the underlying asset price can go.

3. Leverage: As mentioned, buying call options allows you to control a large amount of the underlying asset with a relatively small amount of capital. This means you can magnify your returns if the trade is successful.

Disadvantages of Call Options

However, there are also some disadvantages to using call options:

1. Time Decay: Call options have a limited expiration date, meaning they lose value over time. The longer the expiration date, the more time value an option has. This means that if the underlying asset price does not move in your favor, the option will expire worthless and you will lose the premium paid for the contract.

2. Limited Timeframe: As mentioned, call options have a specific expiration date. This means you need to be correct about the future price movement of the underlying asset within a specific timeframe. If the asset price does not move in your favor before the expiration date, the option will expire worthless.

3. No Ownership Rights: Call option holders have no ownership rights to the underlying asset. They only have the right to buy the asset at a specified price. This means you cannot receive dividends or attend shareholder meetings.

Call options can be a powerful tool for investors looking to speculate, hedge, generate income, or leverage their investments. However, they do come with risks and limitations that investors should be aware of before incorporating them into their investment strategy. It is important to understand how call options work, why investors use them, and their advantages and disadvantages before trading them in the financial market.

Chapter 3: Understanding Put Options

When it comes to investing, there are many different financial instruments to choose from. From stocks to bonds to commodities, there is no shortage of options. One tool that investors can use to hedge their portfolios or speculate on market declines is the put option.

In this chapter, we will explore the basics of put options, including what they are, how they work, and the risks and rewards associated with using them.

What is a Put Option?

A put option is a financial contract that gives the holder the right, but not the obligation, to sell a specific asset (such as a stock) at a predetermined price (the strike price) within a specific period of time (the expiration date). In exchange for this right, the holder pays a premium to the option seller.

Think of a put option as insurance. Just like you might buy car insurance to protect yourself in case of an accident, an investor might buy a put option to protect themselves against a decline in the value of their portfolio.

For example, let's say you own 100 shares of XYZ stock, which is currently trading at $50 per share. You're worried that the stock might decline in value over the next few months, but you don't want to sell your shares just yet. One way to protect yourself is to buy a put option with a strike price of $45 and an expiration date of three months from now. If the stock declines below $45, you can exercise your option and sell your shares for that price, instead of the lower market price.

How Do Put Options Work?

Now that we understand what a put option is, let's dive a bit deeper into how they work.

First, let's look at the different parties involved in a put option contract. The buyer of the put option is called the holder, while the seller is known as the writer. The holder pays a premium to the writer, and in exchange gains the right to sell the underlying asset at the strike price.

Let's continue with our XYZ stock example. You, as the holder, buy a put option with a strike price of $45 and an expiration date of three months from now. You pay a premium of $3 per share, or $300 total (since options contracts typically cover 100 shares). The writer of the option, also known as the seller, receives this premium and agrees to buy the stock from you at the strike price of $45, if you exercise your option.

Now, let's look at what happens if the stock declines in value. Let's say that XYZ stock drops to $40 per share over the next two months. Since your strike price is $45, you can exercise your option and sell your shares for that price, even though the market price is lower. You can now realize a profit of $45 - $40 = $5 per share, or $500 total (100 shares x $5 profit per share).

On the other hand, if the stock remains above the strike price, your option will expire worthless. In this case, you would lose the entire premium that you paid for the option.

Risks and Rewards of Using Put Options

As with any investment, there are risks and rewards associated with using put options. Let's take a closer look at both.

Rewards

The primary reward of using put options is the ability to hedge your portfolio against market declines. By buying put options, you can protect yourself against losses in your underlying assets, while still maintaining your exposure to any potential gains.

In addition to portfolio hedging, put options can also be used for speculative purposes. If you have reason to believe that a particular stock or market is going to decline in value, you can buy put options to profit from that decline.

Another advantage of put options is the leverage that they provide. Since options contracts typically cover 100 shares, you can gain exposure to a larger dollar amount of stocks for a fraction of the cost of buying the shares outright. In our XYZ stock example, you paid $300 for the option, instead of $5,000 for the 100 shares of stock.

Risks

The primary risk of using put options is the potential loss of the premium that you paid for the option. If the stock remains above the strike price, your option will expire worthless, and you will lose the entire premium that you paid.

Another risk of using put options is the limited time frame in which you have to exercise your option. If the stock declines in value, but not enough to reach your strike price before the expiration date, your option will expire worthless, and you will lose the entire premium that you paid.

Finally, it's important to consider the impact of volatility on your put options. Just like with any option, the price of put options is affected by changes in volatility. If volatility increases, the price of the option may increase as well, even if the underlying asset hasn't changed in value. This can make it more expensive to buy put options, cutting into your potential profits.

Put options are a useful tool for investors to protect their portfolios against market declines or to profit from a decline in a particular stock or market. They provide a way to gain exposure to a larger dollar amount of stocks for a fraction of the cost of buying the shares outright, and they offer leverage and flexibility.

However, it's important to understand the risks involved with using put options, including the potential loss of the premium that you paid, the limited time frame in which you have to exercise your option, and the impact of volatility on the price of the option.

Overall, put options can be a valuable addition to your investment toolkit, but they should be used carefully and with a thorough understanding of how they work.

Chapter 4: Basics of Stock Market

The stock market is one of the most fascinating and yet, intimidating investment options for many people. Historically, people have always been drawn to the stock market as a way to accumulate wealth. Even though the stock market can seem very complex and intimidating, it is not as difficult to understand as you might think. In this chapter, we will provide a comprehensive overview of the basics of the stock market, including its history, terminology, and key functions.

History of the Stock Market

The stock market has a long and interesting history that dates back to the 17th century. In the early days, merchants and traders used to gather in coffeehouses in London and Amsterdam to buy and sell shares in trading companies. Over time, this practice became more organized, and the first stock exchange was officially established in Amsterdam in 1720.

In the US, the first stock exchange was founded in Philadelphia in 1790. In 1817, the New York Stock Exchange (NYSE) was created. The NYSE quickly became the most popular stock exchange in the world, and today, it is still considered to be one of the most important stock exchanges in the world.

The Function of the Stock Market

The stock market plays a critical role in the economy. By providing a platform for buying and selling shares in public companies, the stock market enables companies to raise funds for their business operations. It also provides investors with an opportunity to own a piece of a company and potentially make a profit.

When investors buy shares in a company, they become part owners of that company. As the company grows and becomes more profitable, the value of the shares may increase, providing investors with a profit if they sell their shares.

Stock Market Terminology

Understanding the terminology used in the stock market is essential to understanding its functions and processes. Here are some of the most common terms used in the stock market:

- Stock: A share in ownership of a company.

- Shareholder: A person or entity that owns shares in a company.

- Dividend: A payment made by a company to its shareholders. Dividends are usually paid out of a company's profits.

- Bull market: A market in which stock prices are rising.

- Bear market: A market in which stock prices are falling.

- Initial Public Offering (IPO): The first time that a company's shares are sold to the public.

- Market capitalization: The total value of a company's outstanding shares.

Investing in the Stock Market

Investing in the stock market can be a daunting task, but there are a few key things to keep in mind that can help simplify the process. Here are some tips for investing in the stock market:

1. Determine your investment goals: Before you start investing, it's essential to determine your investment goals. Are you looking to make a quick profit, or are you investing for the long-term?

2. Develop an investment plan: Once you've determined your investment goals, develop a plan for how you will achieve them. Your plan should include what stocks you're going to invest in, how much you're going to invest, and how long you plan to hold your investments.

3. Do your research: Before you invest in any stock, do your research. Look at the company's financial statements, annual reports, and any news or headlines related to the company. You should also research the market and industry in which the company operates.

4. Diversify your portfolio: Diversification is an essential aspect of investing in the stock market. Diversifying your portfolio means investing in a variety of different stocks to reduce your risk.

5. Monitor your investments: Finally, it's essential to monitor your investments regularly. Keep an eye on the stock market and any news related to your investments. If something changes that could impact your investments, be prepared to make adjustments to your portfolio.

The stock market may seem like an intimidating place, but by understanding the basics, you can start investing with confidence. The stock market plays a critical role in the economy, providing companies with a platform for raising funds and investors with an opportunity to make a profit. By developing an investment plan, conducting research, diversifying your portfolio, and monitoring your investments, you can start building wealth through the stock market.

Chapter 5: How Options Pricing Works

Options are a type of financial instrument that provide an investor with the right, but not the obligation, to buy or sell an underlying asset at a specified price on or before a certain date. Options can be used to hedge against potential losses or to make speculative investments. As with any financial instrument, the price of an option is determined by supply and demand in the market, as well as factors such as the underlying asset's price, time until expiration, and volatility.

Options come in two varieties: calls and puts. A call option gives the buyer the right, but not the obligation, to buy an underlying asset at a specified price (the strike price) on or before a certain date (the expiration date). A put option, on the other hand, gives the buyer the right, but not the obligation, to sell an underlying asset at a specified price (again, the strike price) on or before a certain date (the expiration date).

The price of an option is known as the premium. This premium is determined by a number of factors, including the underlying asset's price, the option's strike price, the time remaining until expiration, and the volatility of the underlying asset. Let's explore each of these factors in more detail.

Underlying Asset Price

The price of the underlying asset is often the most important factor in determining the price of an option. Generally speaking, call options will increase in price as the price of the underlying asset increases, while put options will increase in price as the price of the underlying asset decreases. This makes intuitive sense - a call option gives the buyer the right to buy an underlying asset at a specified price, so as the price of that asset goes up, so too does the potential profit from exercising the option. Similarly, a put option gives the buyer the right to sell an underlying asset at a specified price, so as the price of that asset goes down, so too does the potential profit from exercising the option.

Strike Price

The strike price of an option is the price at which the underlying asset can be bought or sold. This price is set when the option is initially issued, and is often based on the current market price of the underlying asset. Generally speaking, call options with strike prices below the current market price of the underlying asset will be more expensive, while put options with strike prices above the current market price will be more expensive. This makes sense - if a call option is "in the money" (meaning the strike price is less than the current market price of the underlying asset), there is a higher likelihood that the option will be exercised, and therefore a higher demand for that option. The same principle applies to put options - if a put option is "in the money" (meaning the strike price is greater than the current market price of the underlying asset), there is a higher likelihood that the option will be exercised, and therefore a higher demand for that option.

Time Until Expiration

The amount of time remaining until an option's expiration date is another important factor in determining the price of an option. Generally speaking, the longer the time until expiration, the more expensive the option will be. This is because a longer expiration period gives the buyer more time to potentially profit from exercising the option. For example, if you buy a call option with a strike price of $50 and an expiration date of six months from now, you have six months to potentially profit if the price of the underlying asset goes up. On the other hand, if you buy a call option with the same strike price but an expiration date of only one week from now, your potential profit window is much smaller.

Volatility

Finally, volatility is another important factor in option pricing. Volatility refers to how much the price of the underlying asset is expected to fluctuate over the course of the option's lifespan. Generally speaking, the more volatile the underlying asset, the more expensive the option will be. This makes sense - if an underlying asset is very volatile, there is a higher likelihood that the price will move significantly in one direction or the other, potentially resulting in a larger profit from exercising the option.

In addition to these four primary factors, there are a number of other, more complex factors that can also impact option pricing. These might include factors like interest rates, dividend payouts, and even the options market itself. Some investors use sophisticated mathematical models to try to predict how these various factors will interact and impact option prices.

Overall, option pricing can be a highly complex and nuanced process, with a large number of factors to take into account. For this reason, it's generally a good idea for individual investors to work with a financial advisor or other professional who has experience with options trading. Additionally, it's important to remember that options trading can be inherently risky, and should only be pursued by those who have the financial means to withstand potential losses.

Chapter 6: Reading an Option Chain

Option trading is an advanced investment strategy that allows traders to buy or sell the right to buy or sell a specific underlying asset at a predetermined price. Options trading offers more flexibility, higher potential returns, and lower risks compared to traditional stock trading. Option contracts are traded on Options Exchanges like the Chicago Board Options Exchange (CBOE) or the International Securities Exchange (ISE). The option chain provides comprehensive information and data needed before making an informed trading decision.

Understanding the Option Chain

An option chain is a detailed list of all available options for a particular stock or exchange-traded fund (ETF) for a specific expiration date. The option chain typically contains critical information on each option, including the strike price, the option's expiration date, the bid-ask spread, and other essential information about the contract.

The option chain is the heart of options trading, providing information regarding the options available for trading. It contains option data that traders use to analyze the risk and reward of trading strategies. Therefore, every trader needs to have a good understanding of the option chain and how to interpret the data in it.

The Strike Price

The strike price of an option is the price at which an option buyer can buy or sell the underlying asset. This is also referred to as the exercise price of the option contract. The strike price is an essential variable when it comes to options trading. The buyer of the option is not obligated to buy or sell the underlying security at the strike price. They only have the option to do so before the expiration date of the contract.

Therefore, strike prices are generally categorized as out-of-the-money (OTM), at-the-money (ATM), or in-the-money (ITM). An option is out of the money if the current stock price is not at or near the strike price. An option is said to be at the money when the current stock price is the same as the strike price. Finally, an option is said to be in the money when the current stock price is more than the strike price.

An option buyer may choose an OTM option when they anticipate the stock price will increase, an ITM option when they expect the stock price to go down, or an ATM option when they are uncertain about the stock price movement.

Expiration Date

The expiration date is the deadline when an option contract must be exercised. Once this date passes, the option becomes worthless. An option buyer must exercise the option before the expiration date, or it may lapse, losing its value.

The expiration date in the option chain is represented in the format of month/day/year. The option chain provides an expiration date for each option contract listed. The expiration date gives traders an idea of the timeframe before they must take action on their options trading strategy.

Option Type

The option chain lists call options and put options separately. The call options give the buyer the right to purchase the underlying stock at a specific price (i.e., the strike price) before the expiration date. On the other hand, a put option provides the buyer with the right to sell the underlying stock at the specified strike price before the expiration date.

Call options are usually bought when the trader anticipates the stock price to go up. Conversely, put options are often bought when the trader expects the stock price to go down.

Bid and Ask

The bid and ask prices are essential variables when determining the profitability of an options trade. The bid price is the highest price that a buyer is willing to pay for the option, while the ask price is the lowest price a seller is willing to accept for the option. The bid and ask prices are listed for each option contract in the option chain.

The bid-ask spread is the difference between the bid and ask prices for a specific option. The bid-ask spread plays a crucial role in determining the profitability of the trading strategy since the wider the spread, the more of a disadvantage the buyer is at when purchasing an option.

Volume and Open Interest

The volume and open interest variables in the option chain provide insight into the trading activity for a specific option. The volume refers to the number of contracts traded in a particular option during a particular trading day. High volume indicates high demand and interest in buying and selling the option.

The open interest refers to the number of contracts that are held by traders at a specific point in time. The open interest provides a snapshot of the number of contracts that are outstanding. It represents the total number of long positions in a particular option.

Implied Volatility

Implied volatility provides insight into a particular option's price and potential profit or loss. It measures the market's expectation of the underlying asset's price movement. When the implied volatility is high, traders anticipate large price swings in the underlying stock price. Conversely, low implied volatility suggests a low expectation of price swings.

The option chain provides the implied volatility as an estimated percentage. This number is used to determine the option's fair price, with high implied volatility translating into higher option premiums.

The option chain is an essential resource for traders interested in options trading. It provides comprehensive data on each option available for trading, including the strike price, expiration date, option type, bid and ask prices, volume, open interest, and implied volatility.

Traders need to understand each variable in the option chain since it can significantly impact their trading strategies' profitability. A good understanding of the option chain can help traders make informed decisions and avoid costly mistakes.

Chapter 7: Options Trading Terminology

Aspiring traders who want to learn how to trade options must familiarize themselves with the options trading terminology. Just like any other market or industry, options trading has its own language, which might be confusing to new traders. However, learning the terminology is an essential part of becoming a successful options trader. In this chapter, we will cover some of the critical options trading terminology that traders should know.

Option

Before diving into the different types of options, it's essential to understand what an option is. An option is a contract that provides its owner with the right, but not the obligation, to buy or sell an underlying asset at a specific price and on or before a particular date. The underlying asset can be anything from stocks, indices, commodities, and even currencies.

Call Option

A call option is a contract that gives the owner the right, but not the obligation, to buy an underlying asset at a predetermined price, known as the strike price, on or before a specific date. If the owner chooses not to exercise the call option, the contract expires worthless, and the owner loses the premium paid.

Put Option

A put option is a contract that gives the owner the right, but not the obligation, to sell an underlying asset at a predetermined price, known as the strike price, on or before a specific date. If the owner chooses not to exercise the put option, the contract expires worthless, and the owner loses the premium paid.

Strike Price

The strike price, also known as the exercise price, is the price at which the underlying asset can be bought or sold when the option is exercised. Strike prices can be set at any price level, depending on the perceived market volatility and the expiration date of the option.

Expiration Date

The expiration date is the date on which the option contract expires. After this date, the option is no longer valid, and the owner loses the right to buy or sell the underlying asset.

In-the-Money

An option is said to be in-the-money if it has intrinsic value. A call option is in-the-money if the market price of the underlying asset is higher than the strike price, and a put option is in-the-money if the market price of the underlying asset is lower than the strike price.

Out-of-the-Money

An option is said to be out-of-the-money if it has no intrinsic value. A call option is out-of-the-money if the market price of the underlying asset is lower than the strike price, and a put option is out-of-the-money if the market price of the underlying asset is higher than the strike price.

At-the-Money

An option is said to be at-the-money if its strike price is equal to the market price of the underlying asset. At-the-money options have no intrinsic value and only contain time value.

Option Premium

The option premium is the price paid by the option buyer to the option seller for the right to buy or sell the underlying asset. Factors that impact the option premium include the intrinsic value, time value, market volatility, interest rates, and supply and demand.

Intrinsic Value

The intrinsic value of an option is the difference between the market price of the underlying asset and the strike price. In-the-money options have intrinsic value, while out-of-the-money options have no intrinsic value.

Time Value

Time value is the value of an option that is derived from the time remaining until the option expires. The longer the time until expiration, the higher the time value of an option. Time value diminishes as the option approaches its expiration date.

Volatility

Volatility is the measure of the amount by which the price of an underlying asset is expected to fluctuate in a given period. Higher volatility implies greater potential price swings, which means that options prices typically increase when volatility increases.

Implied Volatility

Implied volatility is the level of volatility that the market is pricing into an option's premium. Implied volatility is an essential component of option trading as it helps traders evaluate the potential for future price swings in the underlying asset and adjust their trading strategies accordingly.

Delta

Delta is the measure of an option's sensitivity to changes in the price of the underlying asset. Delta ranges from 0 to 1 for call options and -1 to 0 for put options. An option with a delta of 0.5 will increase or decrease in value by 50 cents for every dollar move in the underlying asset.

Gamma

Gamma is the measure of an option's sensitivity to changes in delta. Gamma is the rate of change of delta relative to a change in the price of the underlying asset. Gamma is at its highest for at-the-money options and decreases as the option moves further in or out of the money.

Theta

Theta is the measure of an option's time decay. Theta is the rate at which the option's premium decreases as the option nears its expiration date. In general, options with less time until expiration have a higher theta than those with more time until expiration.

Vega

Vega is the measure of an option's sensitivity to changes in implied volatility. Vega is the rate at which an option's premium changes relative to a one-point increase or decrease in implied volatility.

Options trading terminology can be overwhelming and confusing at first, but it is essential to have a solid understanding to become a successful options trader. By following the guide above, you should have a better understanding of the most critical options trading terminology. However, this is just the beginning, and there is much more to learn. Experienced traders will continue to expand their options trading vocabulary and knowledge throughout their trading careers.

Chapter 8: Intrinsic Value and Time Value

In the world of finance, the concept of intrinsic value and time value is one of the most fundamental and important concepts that any investor should know. These two concepts play a critical role in understanding the true worth of an investment asset such as stocks, bonds, commodities, and real estate. The intrinsic value refers to the inherent worth of an asset, while the time value represents the potential future worth of that asset.

In this chapter, we will explore the meaning and principles behind intrinsic value and time value and how they can help investors make informed investment decisions.

The Meaning of Intrinsic Value

The concept of intrinsic value is rooted in the principle of value investing, an investment strategy that focuses on identifying undervalued companies that have strong financials and good fundamentals. The principle of intrinsic value states that an asset is worth only what it can generate in future cash flows, discounted to the present value.

In other words, intrinsic value represents the true worth of an asset and is based on the underlying economic and financial fundamentals of the asset. It is determined by factors such as the company's revenue growth, earnings potential, dividend payouts, and other intrinsic factors that affect the cash flows generated by the asset.

For example, let's say a company's stock is currently trading at $20 per share. The intrinsic value of the stock may be calculated by assessing the company's financial health, including its revenue growth, debt-to-equity ratio, and the overall economic climate, among other factors. If the intrinsic value of the stock is determined to be $30 per share, then the stock is considered undervalued, and there may be a potential opportunity for investors to purchase the stock at a lower price and earn a profit as the stock price rises to its true intrinsic value.

The Principles of Intrinsic Value

There are several important principles that underpin the concept of intrinsic value. These principles play a vital role in determining the intrinsic value of an asset and include the following:

1. Cash Flow: The value of an asset is ultimately based on the cash flows it generates over time. Therefore, the cash flow is a critical factor in determining the intrinsic value of an asset.

2. Risk: The risk associated with an asset is another critical factor in determining its intrinsic value. The higher the risk associated with an asset, the lower its intrinsic value.

3. Time: The duration of cash flows associated with an asset also has

a significant impact on its intrinsic value. The longer the duration of the cash flows, the lower the intrinsic value of the asset.

4. Assets in Place vs. Growth Assets: Assets in place refer to assets that generate consistent cash flows over time, such as mature stocks and bonds, while growth assets refer to assets that have the potential for significant future growth, such as start-up companies. The intrinsic value of growth assets tends to be more difficult to estimate, as it relies on future expectations.

The Meaning of Time Value

Time value is the concept that asset value changes over time. In other words, the value of an asset is a function of its cash flow and the expected interest rate, which in turn impacts the value of the cash flow over time. The time value of an asset is the additional value that investors assign to an asset based on its potential for appreciation, depreciation, and the time it takes for those changes to occur.

In practical terms, time value is the effect of the time remaining until expiration or the end of the investment period, the volatility of the asset, and the risk-free rate. The longer the duration of an investment or the greater the uncertainty about its future, the higher the time value.

The Principles of Time Value

There are several key principles that underpin the concept of time value, including the following:

1. Interest Rates: Interest rates play a critical role in determining the time value of an asset. As interest rates change, the present value of future cash flows changes as well. The higher the interest rate, the lower the present value of future cash flows, and vice versa.

2. Volatility: The more volatile an asset, the higher its time value. This is because the potential for significant appreciation or depreciation is higher, making the asset more attractive to investors.

3. Time to Maturity: The longer the duration of an investment, the greater the time value. This is because the longer the investment period, the greater the potential for appreciation or depreciation.

4. Risk-Free Rate: The risk-free rate is the rate of return on an investment that has zero risk of loss. It is an essential factor in determining the time value of an asset, as it serves as a benchmark or baseline to compare against other investments.

Intrinsic Value vs. Time Value

While intrinsic value and time value are two distinct concepts, they are interconnected and play an essential role in investment decision-making. Intrinsic value is based on the underlying fundamentals of an asset, while time value is based on its potential for appreciation or depreciation over time.

For example, a company with strong fundamentals and a low risk profile may have a high intrinsic value that is not likely to change significantly over time. Conversely, a company with high growth potential but erratic revenue streams may have a lower intrinsic value but a higher time value, as its potential for future growth is high.

Determining the intrinsic value and time value of an asset requires a thorough understanding of its financials, economic conditions, and market trends. Investors need to consider both factors when making investment decisions, as they can impact the potential for profit and the overall risk of the investment.

Intrinsic value and time value are two of the most important concepts that investors should understand when it comes to assessing the potential worth of an investment asset. While intrinsic value is based on the underlying fundamentals of an asset, time value is based on its potential for appreciation or depreciation over time.

Investors need to consider these factors when making investment decisions, as they can impact the potential for profit and the overall risk of the investment. Ultimately, understanding the principles behind intrinsic value and time value is critical for any investor looking to make informed investment decisions and manage their portfolio effectively.

Chapter 9: Introduction to Option Greeks

Options trading is a complex and dynamic activity that requires a thorough understanding of various concepts and techniques. One of the most important concepts in options trading is the "Greeks," which are a set of measures that help traders understand the behavior of their options positions and the effects of various factors on these positions.

The term "Greeks" refers to a set of mathematical variables that are used to measure the sensitivity of options prices to different factors. These factors include changes in the price of the underlying asset, changes in the volatility of the underlying asset, changes in interest rates, and changes in the time to expiration of the options. Knowing the Greeks of an option contract can help traders manage their risks and develop effective strategies for trading options.

In this chapter, we will discuss the most commonly used Greeks in options trading and explain how they are calculated and used. We will also provide some examples of how traders can use these Greeks to manage their positions effectively.

Delta

Delta is perhaps the most widely used Greek in options trading. It measures the sensitivity of the option price to changes in the price of the underlying asset. Delta ranges from 0 to 1 for call options and from -1 to 0 for put options. The closer the delta is to 1 or -1, the more sensitive the option price is to changes in the underlying asset price.

For call options, a delta of 0.5 means that for every $1 increase in the underlying asset price, the call option price will increase by $0.50. For put options, a delta of -0.5 means that for every $1 increase in the underlying asset price, the put option price will decrease by $0.50.

Gamma

Gamma measures the rate of change of delta in response to changes in the underlying asset price. Gamma is therefore an important measure of the options' convexity, that is, how the option price changes in relation to changes in the underlying asset price.

Gamma is highest when the option is at the money, that is, when the strike price is close to the current price of the underlying asset. As the option gets deeper in the money or out of the money, gamma decreases.

Vega

Vega measures the sensitivity of the option price to changes in the volatility of the underlying asset. Vega is highest for at-the-money options and decreases as the options get deeper in the money or out of the money.

Higher Vega means that the option price is more sensitive to changes in volatility, while lower Vega means that the option price is less sensitive to changes in volatility. Vega is usually expressed in dollars, that is, how much the option price will change for a 1% change in the volatility of the underlying asset.

Theta

Theta measures the rate of time decay of the option price as the time to expiration approaches. Theta is usually expressed in dollars, that is, how much the option price will change per day as the time to expiration approaches.

Theta is highest for at-the-money options and decreases as the options get deeper in the money or out of the money. As the option gets closer to expiration, theta increases, indicating that the time value of the option is decreasing.

Rho

Rho measures the sensitivity of the option price to changes in interest rates. Rho is usually expressed in dollars, that is, how much the option price will change for a 1% change in interest rates.

Rho is highest for options with long expiration dates, as changes in interest rates have a greater impact on these options. Rho is usually not a significant factor in short-term options trading, but it can be important for longer-term options trading.

Using Option Greeks

Option Greeks are important tools that traders can use to manage their options positions effectively. By understanding the behavior of their options positions in relation to various factors such as changes in the underlying asset price, volatility, time decay, and interest rates, traders can develop effective strategies for trading options.

For example, if a trader is bullish on a particular stock, they might consider buying a call option with a high delta and a low theta, as this would give them the most exposure to the stock's price movement while minimizing the impact of time decay on the option price. Alternatively, if a trader thinks that a stock might be volatile in the near future, they might consider buying an option with a high Vega, as this would allow them to benefit from any increase in volatility.

Traders can also use option Greeks to manage their risks by hedging their positions. For example, if a trader has a long call option position with a high delta, they might hedge their position by simultaneously selling a futures contract on the underlying asset. This would create a delta-neutral position, which would minimize the impact of changes in the underlying asset price on the trader's overall position.

Option Greeks are important measures that traders use to understand the behavior of their options positions and develop effective trading strategies. Delta, gamma, Vega, theta, and Rho are the most commonly used Greeks, and each measures the sensitivity of the option price to different factors such as changes in the underlying asset price, volatility, time decay, and interest rates.

By understanding the Greeks of their options positions, traders can manage their risks and develop effective strategies for trading options. Traders can also use option Greeks to hedge their positions and minimize the impact of changes in the underlying asset price on their overall position.

Chapter 10: Understanding Delta

Delta is one of the "Greeks" used in options trading. The Greeks are a set of key measures that describe how the price of an option changes in response to various factors. In the case of Delta, it is a measure of how the price of an option changes for every $1 change in the underlying asset's price.

Here's a more detailed explanation:

Delta Value: The delta of an option ranges between 0 and 1 for call options, and -1 and 0 for put options. When the underlying asset increases by $1, the price of a call option will increase by the delta amount. Conversely, for a put option, if the underlying asset increases by $1, the price of the put option will decrease by its delta amount. For example, if a call option has a delta of 0.6, the price of the option would theoretically increase by 60 cents if the underlying asset's price increases by $1.

At, In, and Out of the Money: Delta also gives you a rough measure of the likelihood that an option will end up in-the-money at expiration. For instance, a call option with a delta of 0.7 has approximately a 70% chance of being in-the-money at expiration. Similarly, a call option with a delta of 0.2 has roughly a 20% chance of being in-the-money at expiration.

Delta and Directional Exposure: Delta is also used to gauge the directional exposure of an option. If you're long a call option with a delta of 0.6, your position will behave similarly to being long 60 shares of the underlying stock (since each options contract is for 100 shares). This is helpful for traders to understand how much market exposure they have through their options positions.

Delta Hedging: Some traders use delta to hedge their positions. Delta hedging involves making trades that offset the delta of a position. For example, if you have a call option with a delta of 0.5 on a certain stock, you could hedge your position by shorting 50 shares of the same stock.

Delta and Time Decay: Delta isn't constant. As the underlying asset's price moves or as time passes, the delta of an option changes—a concept known as "gamma." As an option moves more in-the-money or out-of-the-money, or as it gets closer to expiration, its delta will change.

Delta Neutral Strategies: In option trading, a delta neutral strategy involves setting up a portfolio so that the total delta among the assets within it sums to zero. Traders do this to reduce the directional risk associated with price movements in the underlying asset. A delta neutral portfolio could consist of multiple positions with positive and negative deltas that offset each other.

Impacts of Volatility on Delta: When the volatility of the underlying asset increases, the delta of at-the-money (ATM) options tends to get closer to 0.5, whereas the deltas of deep in-the-money (ITM) and deep out-of-the-money (OTM) options tend to move away from 1.0 and 0, respectively. This happens because when volatility is high, the likelihood of dramatic price swings increases, and thus, the likelihood that the option will move ITM or OTM increases.

Long-Term vs. Short-Term Options: Short-term options tend to have larger delta changes than long-term options. This is because the price of a short-term option is more sensitive to changes in the underlying asset's price.

Delta and Dividends: Expected dividends can also impact an option's delta. If the underlying asset is expected to pay a dividend, call deltas can decrease, and put deltas can increase as the ex-dividend date approaches. This is because the stock price usually drops by approximately the dividend amount on the ex-dividend date.

Dynamic Delta: As mentioned earlier, an option's delta changes as the price of the underlying asset changes, a characteristic known as gamma. This means that an option's delta is dynamic, not static. If you are managing a portfolio of options, you need to continually adjust your positions to maintain your desired level of delta exposure.

In summary, understanding the concept of delta in options trading is a critical skill for managing risk and making informed decisions. Keep in mind that delta, like all the Greeks, is a theoretical concept. Real-world results can and often do vary from the theoretical predictions due to factors like changing volatility, liquidity issues, and changes in interest rates.

Chapter 11: Understanding Gamma

Gamma is another one of the "Greeks" used in options trading to measure the sensitivity of an option's delta in relation to the price of the underlying asset. In other words, gamma is the rate of change of an option's delta for a $1 change in the price of the underlying asset. It's essentially the acceleration of an option's price.

Here's a more detailed look at gamma:

Gamma and Delta: As explained before, delta measures the rate of change of an option's price with respect to changes in the price of the underlying asset. However, this rate of change is not constant and can vary as the price of the underlying asset changes. Gamma measures this rate of change of the delta itself. If the gamma of an option is high, the delta can change rapidly, which means the price of the option is highly sensitive to changes in the price of the underlying asset.

Gamma Peak: Gamma is usually highest for at-the-money (ATM) options and smallest for deep-in-the-money (ITM) or deep-out-of-the-money (OTM) options. This means that ATM options will see the most significant change in delta for a $1 move in the underlying asset. Conversely, the deltas for ITM or OTM options won't change as much for a $1 move in the underlying asset.

Gamma and Time Decay: Gamma increases as the expiration date of an option gets closer. This is because as expiration approaches, the price of the option becomes more sensitive to changes in the underlying asset's price.

Gamma and Volatility: Options on volatile assets tend to have lower gammas because their deltas are less stable. Conversely, options on less volatile assets have higher gammas because their deltas are more stable.

Gamma and Option Strategies: Understanding gamma is especially important when employing complex options strategies that involve multiple options, such as spreads, straddles, or strangles. In these cases, the net gamma of the total position matters because it affects how the position's delta changes in response to price movements in the underlying asset.

Gamma Hedging: Some traders use a strategy called gamma hedging to help manage the risk of changes in delta. This strategy involves adjusting a portfolio to achieve a gamma of zero, which makes the delta of the portfolio also stable, reducing the risk associated with price movements in the underlying asset.

Gamma Scalping: This is another trading strategy that involves adjusting a portfolio to capitalize on large price swings in the underlying asset. Traders who use gamma scalping are indifferent to the direction of the market; they make profits from the changes in the price of the option as the price of the underlying asset fluctuates.

Gamma and Theta Interplay: In addition to the relationship between gamma and delta, there is also an important relationship between gamma and theta. As gamma increases, theta also tends to increase. That's because when the delta of an option is more sensitive to the underlying asset price changes (high gamma), the option's time decay (theta) is also more pronounced. This interplay can significantly impact an option's price, especially as the option nears expiration.

Long-Term vs. Short-Term Options: Long-term options tend to have smaller gammas compared to short-term options. That's because price movements in the underlying asset have a less immediate impact on the value of long-term options.

Gamma and Risk Management: Understanding gamma is crucial for risk management in options trading. When an option has a high gamma, a small change in the underlying asset's price can have a significant impact on the option's price. Traders need to be aware of their position's gamma to understand and anticipate how price movements in the underlying asset will affect their portfolio.

Gamma and Market Conditions: The value of gamma can indicate market conditions. Generally, a high gamma suggests a volatile market, while a low gamma suggests a less volatile market. Knowing the market conditions can help traders choose the right trading strategy.

Gamma Skew: Gamma skew refers to the situation where options with different strike prices but the same expiration date have different gamma values. A positive gamma skew occurs when out-of-the-money options have higher gammas, while a negative gamma skew occurs when in-the-money options have higher gammas.

Gamma and Liquidity: Liquid options markets tend to have lower gamma values than illiquid markets. This is because in a liquid market, traders can easily adjust their positions in response to changes in the underlying asset's price. In contrast, in illiquid markets, traders may find it more difficult to adjust their positions, leading to higher gamma values.

Gamma is a dynamic and crucial aspect of options trading. It has profound effects on trading strategies and risk management, and its understanding can provide traders with more in-depth insight into market behavior.

Chapter 12: Understanding Theta

Theta measures the rate of decline in the value of an option due to the passage of time. It is also referred to as the time decay of the option. This rate of decline accelerates as the option gets closer to expiration.

Here's a more in-depth look:

Theta and Time Decay: All else being equal, an option loses value over time. This is because as each day passes, the likelihood of a price move in the underlying asset (and therefore a payoff from the option) decreases. This decay in value is quantified by Theta. If an option has a Theta of -0.05, the option's price would decrease by 5 cents per day, all other factors remaining constant.

Theta Values: Theta is typically negative for purchased options since they lose value over time. The further away the expiration date, the slower the time decay and therefore the smaller (less negative) the Theta. As we get closer to the expiration date, time decay accelerates, and Theta gets larger (more negative).

Theta and Moneyness: Theta is usually highest for at-the-money (ATM) options, as these are the options where the uncertainty about ending in the money is highest, and thus time decay is most significant. Deep in-the-money (ITM) or out-of-the-money (OTM) options have smaller Thetas as their value is less susceptible to time decay - a deep ITM option is already likely to be exercised, and a deep OTM option is unlikely to become ITM before expiration.

Theta and Volatility: An increase in implied volatility, all else being equal, will increase the value of an option. However, it will also cause Theta to increase (become more negative), as with higher potential for price swings, each passing day represents a greater opportunity cost.

Theta and Option Sellers: While time decay (Theta) is detrimental to option buyers, it can benefit option sellers. When you sell an option, a negative Theta means that the value of the option decreases every day, bringing the seller closer to realizing the maximum profit, which is the premium received at the time of selling the option.

Theta in Strategies: Many options strategies, such as iron condors, calendar spreads, or covered calls, rely on Theta. They are generally designed to have positive Theta, meaning they benefit from the passage of time, making them popular with options sellers.

Long-Term vs. Short-Term Options: Longer-term options have Theta decay that is less than shorter-term options. Therefore, traders looking to benefit from time decay will often sell short-term options, while those looking to purchase options may look to longer-term options where time decay will be less of a factor, at least initially.

Theta and Interest Rates: Just like the other Greeks, Theta doesn't exist in isolation, and it's influenced by other factors such as interest rates. When interest rates increase, holding onto cash becomes more valuable as compared to holding onto options (since cash can earn interest). Therefore, when interest rates rise, the time decay represented by Theta is likely to increase.

Weekend Theta Decay: One of the interesting characteristics of Theta is that the time decay does not always happen evenly. Over the weekends, when markets are closed, Theta decay tends to be priced in on Friday and on Monday. Some traders refer to this phenomenon as "Weekend Theta," where the option price on Monday is often lower than it should be based on the Friday closing price.

Theta and Gamma: There's an important relationship between Theta and Gamma. An option with a high Gamma will have a high Theta. This is because when an option is sensitive to changes in the underlying asset's price (a high Gamma), it will also be sensitive to time decay (a high Theta).

Negative Theta Strategies vs. Positive Theta Strategies: Strategies with negative Theta mean that every day you hold the position, it will lose value due to time decay, assuming all other factors remain constant. On the other hand, strategies with positive Theta benefit from time decay. The choice between negative and positive Theta strategies often depends on the trader's market outlook and risk tolerance.

Impact of Theta Near Expiration: As the expiration date nears, the impact of Theta becomes more pronounced. Options lose value at an accelerated rate as they approach their expiration date, especially if they're out-of-the-money. This is why understanding and managing Theta risk is so important in options trading.

Understanding Theta and how it affects an option's price is crucial when formulating trading strategies. It's important to consider Theta in the context of your market outlook, timeframe, and the other Greeks to fully understand the risk/reward profile of your options trades.

Chapter 13: Understanding Vega

Vega measures the sensitivity of an option's price to changes in the volatility of the underlying asset.

Here's a more detailed breakdown of Vega:

Vega and Volatility: Vega indicates how much an option's price changes given a 1% change in implied volatility, all other factors being equal. If an option has a Vega of 0.10, for instance, the option's price will increase by $0.10 if the implied volatility increases by 1%, and it will decrease by $0.10 if the implied volatility decreases by 1%.

Vega Values: Vega is always positive, and is usually higher for at-the-money (ATM) options and lower for in-the-money (ITM) and out-of-the-money (OTM) options.

Vega and Time to Expiration: Vega generally increases as the time to expiration increases. This is because the longer the time until an option expires, the more uncertainty there is about what will happen to the price of the underlying asset, making volatility a more significant factor.

Vega and Option Types: Both calls and puts have positive Vega values, meaning they both increase in price with an increase in volatility and decrease in price with a decrease in volatility. This is because higher volatility implies a greater range of potential underlying asset prices, increasing the probability that the option will expire in-the-money.

Vega Risk: Vega represents the risk that changes in volatility pose to an option. An option with a high Vega is more exposed to changes in volatility, meaning its price will change more significantly when volatility changes.

Vega and Volatility Smile: The Vega of options often forms a pattern known as the "volatility smile" when graphed against different strike prices. This pattern shows that Vega is typically highest for ATM options and decreases for both ITM and OTM options.

Vega in Option Strategies: Understanding Vega is crucial when constructing an options strategy, as it allows traders to assess how changes in volatility will affect the price of the options in their portfolio. Certain strategies, such as straddles and strangles, can benefit from an increase in volatility and therefore have positive Vega. Others, such as credit spreads, can benefit from a decrease in volatility and have negative Vega.

Vega and Other Greeks: Vega can also interact with other Greeks. For instance, options with high Vega also tend to have high Gamma. This is because when an option's price is more sensitive to changes in the underlying asset's volatility, it is often also more sensitive to changes in the underlying asset's price.

Vega and Black-Scholes Model: The concept of Vega, like the other Greeks, arises from the Black-Scholes options pricing model. Vega specifically derives from the part of the model that incorporates volatility. In essence, the model tells us that as volatility increases, there's a higher chance of significant price moves, which potentially increases the value of the option - hence the positive Vega.

Vega and Historical Volatility: While Vega measures the sensitivity of an option's price to changes in implied volatility, it doesn't directly consider historical volatility. However, implied volatility often reflects market expectations based on historical volatility. A significant divergence between implied and historical volatility may present trading opportunities.

Vega and Earnings Announcements: Vega often comes into play around earnings announcements or other significant company events. Traders expect these events to increase price volatility, and thus the implied volatility (and the Vega) of the option may increase leading up to the event.

Vega and Skew: The volatility skew, or smile, is a phenomenon in which OTM and ITM options have higher implied volatilities than ATM options. Vega plays a role in this skew because options with different strike prices have different Vegas. A positive skew (higher volatility for OTM options) suggests a higher Vega for these options, while a negative skew suggests a higher Vega for ITM options.

Vega Neutral: Just as a portfolio can be delta neutral, it can also be Vega neutral. A Vega-neutral strategy aims to balance sensitivity to changes in volatility. This is typically achieved by holding long and short positions in options that offset each other's Vega. Such a portfolio should be relatively unaffected by changes in the underlying asset's volatility.

Vega and Interest Rates: While Vega primarily measures sensitivity to volatility, changes in other factors like interest rates can indirectly affect Vega. When interest rates rise, call options generally increase in value, and put options generally decrease in value. This change in option value can alter implied volatility, thus affecting Vega.

Understanding Vega in options trading provides valuable insights into how changes in market volatility can affect an option's price. By managing Vega effectively, traders can better position themselves to profit from shifts in market volatility, or to protect their portfolio from volatility risks.

Chapter 14: Understanding Rho

Rho, another of the "Greeks" in options trading. Rho measures the sensitivity of an option's price to changes in the risk-free interest rate.

Here is a more detailed look at Rho:

Rho and Interest Rates: Rho indicates how much an option's price changes given a 1% change in interest rates. For example, if a call option has a Rho of 0.05, the price of the option will increase by $0.05 if the interest rate increases by 1%, and it will decrease by $0.05 if the interest rate decreases by 1%.

Rho Values: Rho is positive for call options and negative for put options. This is because when interest rates increase, the cost of carrying an asset financed by borrowing (as is implicitly the case when you buy a call option) increases, making the call option more valuable. Conversely, when interest rates decrease, the return on cash (which you would receive sooner with a put option) decreases, making the put option less valuable.

Rho and Time to Expiration: Rho generally increases as the time to expiration increases. This is because the longer the time until an option expires, the greater the impact of changes in interest rates.

Rho Risk: Rho represents the risk that changes in interest rates pose to an option. An option with a high Rho is more exposed to changes in interest rates, meaning its price will change more significantly when interest rates change.

Rho in Option Strategies: Understanding Rho is crucial when constructing an options strategy, as it allows traders to assess how changes in interest rates will affect the price of the options in their portfolio. Certain strategies can benefit from an increase in interest rates and therefore have positive Rho, while others can benefit from a decrease in interest rates and have negative Rho.

Rho and Other Greeks: Rho can also interact with other Greeks. For instance, longer-term options have higher Vegas, and because they're more sensitive to changes in volatility, they're also more sensitive to changes in interest rates, resulting in a higher Rho.

Let's continue with more insights about Rho:

Rho and Dividends: While Rho measures the sensitivity of an option's price to changes in interest rates, it doesn't directly consider dividends. However, higher dividends can decrease the price of a stock, thereby affecting the price of call and put options. Consequently, changes in dividends can indirectly affect Rho.

Rho and Monetary Policy: Rho is especially relevant during periods when interest rates are changing, such as when a central bank is implementing a change in monetary policy. If interest rates are expected to rise, call options may increase in price and put options may decrease in price.

Rho and Zero Interest Rates: In an environment where interest rates are at or near zero (or negative), Rho becomes less relevant because changes in interest rates have minimal impact on the pricing of options.

Rho and Long-Term Options: Rho is typically larger for long-term options because changes in interest rates have a more significant impact on these options. Traders with longer time horizons must therefore pay particular attention to Rho.

Rho and Black-Scholes Model: Like the other Greeks, Rho stems from the Black-Scholes model of options pricing. Rho is derived from the part of the model that considers the risk-free interest rate. In essence, the model implies that as interest rates rise, it becomes costlier to hold a position in an option rather than in the underlying asset, thereby increasing the value of the option and the Rho.

Rho and Risk Management: While Rho is often smaller in magnitude compared to other Greeks for typical options, for very long-dated options, Rho can become quite large and therefore important to consider for risk management. It's essential for traders to understand how a change in interest rates might impact their options' positions, especially in an environment where interest rates are expected to rise.

Rho Neutral: Just like a portfolio can be delta, gamma, vega, or theta neutral, it can also be made Rho neutral. A Rho-neutral strategy would involve balancing a portfolio so that it's not exposed to changes in interest rates. This is typically achieved by holding a mix of positions where the positive and negative Rhos cancel each other out.

Rho and Fixed Income Securities: The concept of Rho is also applicable in the fixed income market, where it measures a bond's sensitivity to interest rate changes. However, the interpretation of Rho in the context of fixed income securities differs slightly from its interpretation in the context of options.

Rho and Economic Indicators: Economic indicators that might signal a change in interest rates can have an indirect impact on Rho. Traders often closely watch economic news and indicators, such as inflation reports, unemployment data, and GDP growth, as these can influence central bank policies and, subsequently, interest rates.

In summary, Rho is a lesser-known but still vital component of the Greeks in options trading. While often overshadowed by the likes of Delta, Gamma, Vega, and Theta, Rho offers essential insight into how changing interest rates can impact an option's price. Particularly for long-term options or in environments with volatile interest rates, Rho can play a significant role in an options portfolio's performance. Therefore, understanding Rho and its implications can be a valuable tool for options traders.

Chapter 15: Buying and Selling Options

Options are derivatives that offer the right but not the obligation to buy or sell an underlying asset, such as a stock, at a specified price and time. Options trading provides investors with the ability to leverage their trades and make profits in both rising and falling markets. Essentially, options are contracts between buyers and sellers that offer flexibility in trading, risk management, and speculation.

In this chapter, we will explore the fundamentals of buying and selling options, including the different types of options, strategies, and factors influencing option prices. We will also discuss the risks and rewards of trading options and how they compare to other investment vehicles.

Types of Options:

There are two types of options: calls and puts. A call option gives the buyer of the option the right to buy an underlying asset at a specific price, known as the strike price, before the option's expiration date. A put option, on the other hand, gives the buyer of the option the right to sell an underlying asset at a specified price before the option's expiration date.

When buying a call option, the investor is bullish or optimistic about the future price of the underlying asset. For instance, if an investor buys a call option on a stock with a strike price of $50 and the stock price rises to $60 at expiration, the investor can exercise the option and buy the stock at the $50 strike price. The investor can then sell the stock at the current market price of $60, making a profit of $10 per share.

When buying a put option, the investor is bearish or pessimistic about the future price of the underlying asset. For example, if an investor buys a put option on a stock with a strike price of $50 and the stock price falls to $40 at expiration, the investor can exercise the option and sell the stock at the $50 strike price. The investor can then buy the stock at the current market price of $40, making a profit of $10 per share.

Option Strategies:

There are many strategies that investors can use to trade options depending on their risk tolerance, market outlook, and investment objectives. Here are some of the most common option strategies:

1. Covered Call Strategy - involves buying an underlying asset and selling a call option on the same asset. This strategy generates income from the premium received from selling the call option.

2. Protective Put Strategy - involves buying an underlying asset and buying a put option on the same asset. This strategy provides protection against losses if the underlying asset's price falls.

3. Straddle Strategy - this involves buying both a call and a put option on the same underlying asset with the same strike price and expiration date. This strategy makes a profit if the underlying asset's price moves significantly in either direction.

4. Butterfly Spread - this involves buying and selling call options and put options with three different strike prices. This strategy generates profit if the underlying asset's price remains within a certain range at expiration.

5. Iron Condor - this involves buying and selling call options and put options with four different strike prices. This strategy generates profit if the underlying asset's price remains within a certain range at expiration.

Factors Influencing Option Prices:

Option prices are influenced by various factors, including:

1. Stock Price – the price of the underlying asset affects the option's price. As the price of the asset rises, so does the call option price, while the put option price falls.

2. Strike Price - the fixed price at which the option can be exercised affects the option's price. Options with lower strike prices (in-the-money) have higher premiums than options with higher strike prices (out-of-the-money).

3. Time to Expiration – as the expiration date approaches, the option's time value decreases. Options with longer expiration dates have higher premiums than options with shorter expiration dates.

4. Volatility - the price volatility of the underlying asset affects the option's price. More volatile assets have higher premiums than less volatile assets.

5. Interest Rates – higher interest rates increase the cost of carrying the underlying asset, which reduces the call option price and increases the put option price.

Risks and rewards of Trading Options:

Like any investment, options trading has its risks and rewards. Here are some of the risks and rewards of trading options:

Risks:

1. Limited Shelf Life - Options have an expiration date, which limits their shelf life. If the option is not exercised before the expiration date, it becomes worthless.

2. Volatility - The price of options is highly sensitive to volatility in the underlying asset. High volatility can lead to greater losses as well as profits.

3. Leverage – options trading involves leverage, which means that a small investment can lead to significant gains or losses. This can result in higher risk exposure.

Rewards:

1. Flexibility - Options trading provides investors with flexibility in trading, risk management, and speculation.

2. High Rewards - Option trades often have the potential for higher returns than conventional trades.

3. Downside Limitation - Options can offer downside protection by limiting the amount of losses that can be incurred.

Buying and selling options are a popular investment strategy that offers investors the opportunity to leverage trades and make a profit in both rising and falling markets. Understanding the basics of options trading is crucial to making informed decisions and maximizing returns. By understanding the different types of options, strategies, and factors influencing option prices, investors can make informed decisions and manage risk effectively. While there are risks associated with options trading, the rewards can be significant with proper risk management and preparation.

Chapter 16: Trading Options on Margin

Trading options on margin has become one of the most popular strategies for experienced traders who are looking to increase their potential profits while minimizing risk. Essentially, trading on margin involves borrowing money from your broker in order to make larger trades than you would be able to with your own capital. This can be an effective tool for generating more profit, but it also carries increased risks that traders need to be aware of.

In this chapter, we'll explore the ins and outs of trading options on margin, including how it works, the risks involved, and some strategies for maximizing your potential profits.

How Does Trading on Margin Work?

When you trade on margin, you essentially borrow money from your broker to make a trade. The amount of money you can borrow depends on the margin requirements set by your broker, which may vary depending on the type of asset you're trading and your level of experience as a trader.

For example, let's say you want to buy 100 shares of a stock that's currently trading at $50 per share. Without margin, you would need to have $5,000 in your account in order to make the trade. However, if your broker offers a 50% margin requirement, you would be able to borrow $2,500 from your broker, allowing you to make the trade with just $2,500 of your own capital.

In exchange for borrowing funds from your broker, you'll be required to pay interest on the margin loan. The interest rates can vary widely, depending on the broker and the type of trade you're making, so it's important to shop around and compare rates before deciding on a broker.

The Risks of Trading on Margin

While trading on margin can be a useful tool for maximizing your potential profits, it also comes with significant risks that traders need to be aware of. Here are a few risks to keep in mind:

1. Increased Losses: One of the biggest risks of trading on margin is that it amplifies your potential losses. If the market moves against you, the losses you incur will be magnified because you've borrowed money to make the trade. This can result in significant financial losses if you're not careful.

2. Margin Calls: When you trade on margin, you'll be required to maintain a certain level of equity in your account at all times. If your account falls below this level, you'll receive a margin call from your broker, requiring you to deposit more funds or liquidate some of your positions to meet the margin requirement. This can be a stressful situation for traders, as it often results in forced selling at unfavorable prices.

3. Volatility: Trading on margin can also be risky because it often involves trading volatile assets. When you trade options on margin, you're essentially increasing your exposure to the underlying asset, which means that even small fluctuations in the price can have a big impact on your profits or losses.

Strategies for Trading Options on Margin

Despite the risks involved, many experienced traders find that trading options on margin can be a profitable strategy if they're careful and disciplined. Here are a few strategies for maximizing your potential profits while minimizing your risk:

1. Use Stop Loss Orders: When trading on margin, it's important to use stop loss orders to limit your potential losses. A stop loss order is an instruction to your broker to sell your position if the price falls below a certain level. This can help you avoid major losses if the market moves against you.

2. Keep Your Positions Small: Another key strategy when trading on margin is to keep your positions small relative to your account balance. This will help you avoid receiving margin calls or being forced to sell at unfavorable prices. A good rule of thumb is to limit each trade to no more than 5% of your account balance.

3. Focus on High-Probability Trades: When trading options on margin, it's important to focus on high-probability trades that have a

higher chance of success. This can help you avoid taking unnecessary risks and increase your chances of generating a profit.

4. Diversify Your Portfolio: Finally, it's important to diversify your portfolio when trading on margin. This means spreading your risk across multiple assets and trading strategies, so that you're not overly exposed to any one particular asset or market. Diversification can help reduce your overall risk and increase your chances of generating consistent profits.

Trading options on margin can be a powerful tool for experienced traders looking to maximize their potential profits. However, it's important to understand the risks involved and to use a disciplined approach to minimize these risks. By following the strategies outlined above, you can increase your chances of success and generate consistent profits while trading on margin.

Chapter 17: Bullish Options Strategies

When it comes to investment strategies, it's essential to have a variety of options available at your disposal. What works in one market situation may not work in another, and it is crucial to be able to adapt to the changing market conditions. Bullish options strategies are one such set of tools available to investors when they believe the market is going to trend upward. In this chapter, we will explore what bullish options strategies are, how they work, and when you should use them.

Bullish Market vs. Bearish Market

Before we delve into bullish options strategies, it is essential to understand market conditions. A bullish market occurs when the stock prices are expected to rise, indicating investor optimism. In a bullish market, buyers outnumber sellers, and stocks tend to have a bullish tone. Since the overall market is moving up, it is easier to make money for investors.

On the other hand, a bearish market is characterized by a downward trend in stock prices, which indicates investor pessimism. In a bear market, sellers outnumber buyers, making it challenging to make profits.

What are Bullish Options Strategies?

Options contracts are financial derivatives that are popular investment tools for traders. It is essential to know that options trading is not a straightforward investment strategy, and it requires knowledge, experience, and risk management. In a nutshell, options are contracts that give buyers the right, but not the obligation to buy or sell an underlying asset at a particular price and date.

A bullish options strategy is a technique used by investors in a bullish market condition, allowing them to profit from an upward trending market. These strategies make use of call options contracts as the primary trading tool.

Call Option

A call option is a financial contract that provides the buyer (holder) the right, but not the obligation to buy an underlying asset (like stocks, commodities or bonds) at a particular price (strike price) at or before a specific date (expiration date). The buyer pays a premium for this opportunity.

The seller of the call option (a.k.a. the option writer) is obligated to sell the asset to the buyer at the strike price if the buyer exercises the option. The seller receives the premium and hopes that the price of the asset will stay below the strike price.

Bullish Options Strategies

There are several bullish options strategies that investors can use in a bullish market. Here are a few of the most popular strategies.

1. Long Call

A long call is a bullish strategy that involves buying a call option contract on an underlying asset. This option gives the buyer the right but not the obligation to buy the underlying asset at a fixed price (strike price) on or before the expiration date.

When an investor believes that a particular stock or asset is going to rise in value over a specific period, they can use a long call strategy to profit. In this case, the investor buys the call option contract at a specific strike price, and if the price of the asset rises above that price, the investor can exercise the option and buy the underlying asset.

The investor can profit from this strategy in the following two ways:

1. If the price of the asset rises above the strike price, the investor can exercise the option and buy the asset at a lower price than market value to sell it at a profit.

2. If the price of the asset stays below the strike price, the investor will only lose the premium they paid for the option.

2. Bull Call Spread

A bull call spread is a strategy that involves buying a call option and simultaneously selling a call option at a higher strike price on the same underlying asset. This strategy is also called a vertical call spread because the two options have different strike prices and are bought and sold simultaneously.

Investors use this strategy when they believe that the price of the underlying asset will rise but want to limit the amount of potential losses. The investor can profit from this strategy in the following two ways:

1. If the price of the asset rises above the lower strike price, the investor can exercise the call option and buy the asset at the lower strike price and sell the higher-priced option at a profit.

2. If the price of the asset stays below the lower strike price, the investor can only lose the premium they paid for the options contract.

3. Bull Put Spread

A bull put spread is a strategy that involves selling a put option and simultaneously buying a put option at a lower strike price on the same underlying asset. This strategy allows investors to participate in the market while limiting their downside risk. This strategy is also called a vertical put spread.

Investors use this strategy when they believe that the price of the underlying asset will remain stable or rise over a specific period. The investor can profit from this strategy in two ways:

1. If the price of the asset rises above the higher strike price, the investor can only earn a maximum profit equal to the premium paid for the options contract.

2. If the price of the asset falls below the lower strike price, the investor can be forced to buy a stock at the lower strike price. However, the profit earned from selling the higher-priced put option will mitigate the loss.

4. Long Call Condor

A long call condor is a more complex strategy that involves four options contracts, two of which are purchased, and two are sold. This strategy is used when the investor believes that the price of the underlying asset will remain stable with a possible upward trend.

The investor can profit from this strategy in the following two ways:

1. If the price of the asset rises above the higher strike price of the call options or remains stable between the two strike prices of the call options, the investor can earn a profit since both options can be

exercised.

2. If the price of the asset decreases below the lower strike price of the call options, the investor will lose the premium paid for the two purchased options.

Bullish options strategies are popular investment strategies used by traders to benefit from price increases in the underlying asset. While the strategies mentioned above can be highly effective, they also come with risks and require careful consideration. As with all investment strategies, it is essential to thoroughly weigh the risks and benefits before making any investment decision. Investors who wish to employ bullish options strategies should also have a sound understanding of options trading and risk management principles.

Chapter 18: Bearish Options Strategies

Bearish options strategies are used to make a profit when the market is expected to go down. Options are financial derivatives that give buyers the right, but not the obligation, to buy or sell an underlying asset at a predetermined price (strike price) and time (expiration date). Option buyers pay a premium to option sellers, who assume the risk of potential losses, if the option is exercised. Option trading is a risky and complex activity that requires knowledge, experience, and discipline. In this chapter, we will explore some bearish options strategies that investors may use to profit from a bearish market or to hedge their existing portfolio.

Put Options

A put option is a bearish bet on a stock or an index. A put option gives the buyer the right to sell an underlying asset at a fixed price (strike price) before a certain date (expiration date). If the market price of the asset is below the strike price at the expiration date, the option buyer can sell the asset at a higher price and make a profit. If the market price is above the strike price, the option buyer may choose not to exercise the option and lose the premium paid.

Put options are useful for hedging, speculating, or arbitraging. Hedgers may buy put options to protect their portfolio from a market downturn. Speculators may buy put options to profit from a decline in the market. Arbitrageurs may buy put options and short sell the underlying asset to capture a price discrepancy between the option and the asset.

Put options have some advantages and disadvantages. The main advantage is that the investor's potential loss is limited to the premium paid, while the potential profit is unlimited. The main disadvantage is that the investor must be right about the direction and timing of the market movement. If the market remains flat or goes up, the put option may expire worthless, and the investor loses the premium paid.

Bear Put Spread

A bear put spread is a strategy that combines the purchase of a put option with a higher strike price and the sale of a put option with a lower strike price. The goal of this strategy is to reduce the cost of the put option by selling a put option with a lower strike price, while limiting the potential profit by capping the downside risk with the higher strike price.

For example, suppose an investor believes that a stock XYZ, currently trading at $50, will decline in the next three months. The investor buys a put option with a strike price of $55, paying a premium of $2 per share. The investor also sells a put option with a strike price of $45, receiving a premium of $1 per share. The net cost of the strategy is $1 per share, or $100 per contract (100 shares). The maximum potential profit is $4 per share or $400 per contract (if the stock goes to zero), and the breakeven point is $54 per share ($55 strike price minus $1 premium paid).

The bear put spread is a conservative strategy that limits the downside risk and the potential profit. The investor benefits from a bearish movement of the market, but also pays a premium for the hedging. The success of this strategy depends on the accuracy of the timing and direction of the market.

Long Put Butterfly

A long put butterfly is a strategy that involves buying a put option with a low strike price, selling two put options with a middle strike price, and buying a put option with a high strike price. The goal of this strategy is to profit from a narrow range of bearish movement in the market, while limiting the losses in case of a wide movement.

For example, suppose an investor believes that a stock XYZ, currently trading at $50, will decline slightly in the next three months. The investor buys a put option with a strike price of $45, paying a premium of $3 per share. The investor sells two put options with a strike price of $47.50, receiving a premium of $1.50 per share each. The investor also buys a put option with a strike price of $50, paying a premium of $0.50 per share. The net cost of the strategy is zero ($100 per contract), and the maximum potential profit is $2 per share or $200 per contract (if the stock closes at $47.50 on expiration). The breakeven points are $42.50 and $52.50 (the strikes minus/plus the net premium received/paid).

The long put butterfly is a complex strategy that offers limited profit potential and limited risk. The investor must be right about both the direction and the range of the market movement to profit from this strategy. This strategy is suitable for experienced traders who have a high tolerance for risk.

Bear Call Spread

A bear call spread is a strategy that involves buying a call option with a high strike price and selling a call option with a lower strike price. The goal of this strategy is to earn a premium from the sale of the call option, while limiting the potential loss by buying a call option with a higher strike price.

For example, suppose an investor believes that a stock XYZ, currently trading at $50, will not rise significantly in the next three months. The investor sells a call option with a strike price of $55, receiving a premium of $2 per share. The investor also buys a call option with a strike price of $60, paying a premium of $1 per share. The net credit of the strategy is $1 per share, or $100 per contract. The maximum potential loss is $4 per share or $400 per contract (if the stock goes above $60), and the breakeven point is $54 per share ($55 strike price plus $1 premium received).

The bear call spread is a conservative strategy that limits the upside risk and the potential profit. The investor benefits from a bearish movement of the market, but also gives up some of the potential profit. The success of this strategy depends on the accuracy of the timing and direction of the market.

Bearish options strategies are tools that investors may use to profit from a bearish market or to hedge their existing portfolio. Put options, bear put spreads, long put butterflies, and bear call spreads are some examples of bearish options strategies that vary in complexity, risk, and potential profit. Each strategy has its advantages and disadvantages and requires knowledge, experience, and discipline to implement. Before investing in options, investors should understand the risks, conduct thorough research, and consult with an experienced broker or financial advisor. Options trading is not suitable for all investors and involves a high degree of risk.

Chapter 19: Neutral Options Strategies

The world of options trading can be complex and challenging, particularly for newcomers to the space. There are many factors to consider, including market trends, volatility, and the potential for losses. One way to navigate this space is by using neutral options strategies - an approach that seeks to profit from limited price movements while minimizing risk exposure. In this guide, we'll explore some of the key concepts and techniques involved in neutral options trading.

What are Neutral Options Strategies?

Neutral options strategies are a set of techniques that aim to generate profits in markets that are experiencing mild to moderate price movements, without taking an aggressive bullish or bearish stance. In other words, these strategies are designed to help traders benefit from sideways or range-bound markets. Neutral options strategies typically involve buying and selling call and put options simultaneously, effectively creating a "neutral" position that isn't biased towards a particular direction.

One of the most popular neutral options strategies is the "Iron Condor," which involves buying and selling both call and put options with different strike prices and expiration dates. This creates a range in which the underlying asset's price can move without impacting the trader's position. If the price of the asset remains within this range until the options expire, the trader can potentially generate a profit.

Another example of a neutral options strategy is the "Butterfly Spread," in which a trader buys and sells call and put options with similar strike prices, but different expiration dates. This creates a position that's neutral to price movements in either direction, with the potential for profit if the price of the underlying asset remains stable.

Other neutral options strategies include the "Long Straddle," which involves buying both a call and a put option at the same strike price and expiration date, and the "Short Strangle," which involves selling call and put options with different strike prices but the same expiration date.

Benefits of Neutral Options Strategies

There are several benefits to employing neutral options strategies, particularly for traders who are looking to minimize risk exposure while still generating profits. Some of the primary advantages of these strategies include:

- Reduced Risk: Neutral options strategies are designed to minimize risk exposure by creating positions that are neutral to market movements. This means that traders can potentially benefit from price changes without incurring excessive losses.

- Flexibility: Neutral options strategies can be tailored to suit different market conditions and individual trader preferences. For example, traders can adjust the strike prices and expiration dates of their options to create positions that are more or less neutral to market movements.

- Limited Losses: Because neutral options strategies involve buying and selling call and put options simultaneously, the potential for losses is limited. Even if the price of the underlying asset moves outside of the range created by the options, the trader's losses are capped at a predetermined amount.

- Potential for Profits: Neutral options strategies have the potential to generate profits even in sideways or range-bound markets. This can be particularly beneficial for traders who prefer to avoid taking a bullish or bearish stance.

Key Considerations

While neutral options strategies can be a useful tool for traders, there are several key considerations to keep in mind. These include:

- Market Volatility: Neutral options strategies are generally less effective in volatile markets, where prices can fluctuate rapidly and unpredictably. Traders should be aware of prevailing market conditions and adjust their strategies accordingly.

- Time Decay: As options near their expiration dates, they begin to lose value. This can impact the profitability of neutral options strategies, as the trader may need to close their position before expiration to avoid significant losses.

- Commission and Fees: Buying and selling options can come with significant commission and fees, which can eat into a trader's profits. Traders should factor these costs into their strategies to ensure profitability.

- Technical Analysis: As with any trading strategy, traders using neutral options strategies should conduct thorough technical analysis to identify potential entry and exit points. This can involve analyzing market trends, support and resistance levels, and other technical indicators.

Neutral options strategies can be a useful tool for traders looking to minimize risk exposure while still generating profits. These strategies are designed to benefit from sideways or range-bound markets without taking an aggressive bullish or bearish stance. They offer several benefits, including reduced risk, flexibility, limited losses, and potential for profits. However, traders should be aware of key considerations such as market volatility, time decay, commission and fees, and technical analysis. By carefully analyzing these factors, traders can develop effective neutral options strategies that allow them to navigate the complex world of options trading with confidence and success.

Chapter 20: Risk Management in Options Trading

Options trading can be extremely lucrative, but it is not without its risks. As with all forms of investment, options trading requires careful risk management to maximize profits and minimize losses. In this chapter, we will explore some of the key strategies and techniques for effective risk management in options trading.

1. Understanding Option Risk

Before we dive into specific risk management strategies, it is important to have a basic understanding of the risks involved in options trading. The primary risk associated with options trading is the potential for loss of capital. Unlike stocks, which can only fall to zero, options can become worthless in an instant. This is because options are contracts that give the holder the right, but not the obligation, to buy or sell an underlying asset at a certain price (the strike price) on or before a specific date (the expiration date). If the underlying asset does not move in the way that the option trader anticipates, the option may expire worthless.

The second major risk associated with options trading is volatility risk. Volatility refers to the degree of price variability of an asset. Higher volatility means that the price of the asset can swing wildly in either direction, while lower volatility means that the price is more stable. Options prices are highly sensitive to changes in volatility, which can either increase or decrease the value of an option.

Therefore, option traders must be aware of the volatility of the underlying asset and adjust their trading strategy accordingly.

2. Risk Management Strategies

Now that we have a basic understanding of the risks involved in options trading, let's turn to some risk management strategies that can help option traders limit their losses and maximize their profits.

a. Basic Options Strategies

The simplest and most effective way to manage risk in options trading is to use basic options strategies. These strategies involve combining options positions to create a risk profile that matches the trader's investment goals. Some of the most popular basic options strategies include:

- Long call: A long call involves buying a call option, which gives the trader the right to buy an underlying asset at a certain price within a specific time frame. This strategy is used when the trader believes that the price of the underlying asset will rise.

- Long put: A long put involves buying a put option, which gives the trader the right to sell an underlying asset at a certain price within a specific time frame. This strategy is used when the trader believes that the price of the underlying asset will fall.

- Covered call: A covered call involves selling a call option on an underlying asset that the trader owns. The trader earns a premium from the sale of the call option, but if the price of the underlying asset rises above the strike price, the trader must sell the asset at a loss.

- Protective put: A protective put involves buying a put option on an underlying asset that the trader owns. The put option provides insurance against a decline in the price of the underlying asset, but it also reduces the potential profit from owning the asset.

b. Hedging Strategies

Another way to manage risk in options trading is to use hedging strategies. Hedging involves taking a position in one asset to offset the risk in another asset. In options trading, hedging strategies involve taking a position in one or more options contracts to offset the risk in an underlying asset. Some of the most common hedging strategies used in options trading include:

- Delta hedging: Delta hedging involves taking an opposing position in an option to offset the risk of the underlying asset. For example, if an option trader owns a call option on a stock, they can hedge their position by shorting the underlying stock. This way, if the price of the stock falls, the trader will make a profit on their short position, which will offset the losses on their call option.

- Gamma hedging: Gamma hedging involves adjusting the position of an option as the underlying asset's price changes. This strategy is used when the trader believes that the underlying asset's price will be highly volatile. Gamma hedging involves buying or selling additional options contracts in response to changes in the underlying asset's price.

c. Position Sizing

Another important risk management strategy in options trading is position sizing. Position sizing refers to the amount of money a trader invests in each trade. Position sizing is important because it determines the maximum amount of risk the trader is willing to take on in each trade. If a trader invests too much in a single trade, they risk losing a substantial amount of their capital if the trade goes bad. On the other hand, if a trader invests too little, they risk missing out on potential profits.

One commonly used method of position sizing is the Kelly criterion. The Kelly criterion is a formula for determining the optimal percentage of capital to invest in a particular trade. The formula takes into account the probability of success, the size of the potential profit, and the size of the potential loss.

d. Stop Loss Orders

Stop loss orders are another important risk management tool in options trading. A stop loss order is an order that automatically sells an underlying asset when it reaches a certain price. Stop loss orders are used to limit losses on a trade and protect the trader's capital. For example, if a trader buys a call option on a stock and sets a stop loss order at 10% below the purchase price, the underlying stock will be sold automatically if the price falls by 10%.

e. Diversification

Finally, diversification is an essential risk management strategy for all forms of investing, including options trading. Diversification involves spreading investments across different assets and asset classes. By diversifying their portfolio, traders reduce their exposure to any single asset or market, which helps to minimize the impact of any losses.

Effective risk management is critical to success in options trading. By understanding the risks involved in options trading, using basic options strategies, implementing hedging strategies, practicing position sizing, setting stop loss orders, and diversifying their portfolio, traders can limit their losses and increase their chances of success.

Chapter 21: Setting Up an Options Trading Account

Options trading can be an exciting and potentially lucrative activity for savvy investors looking to diversify their portfolios. Before getting started with options trading, however, it's important to set up an account with a broker that offers this type of trading. In this chapter, we'll explore the steps involved in setting up an options trading account.

1. Determine your goals

The first step in setting up an options trading account is to determine your goals. What do you hope to achieve through options trading? Are you looking to generate income, hedge against risk, or achieve capital gains? Your answers to these questions will help you determine the types of options you should trade, as well as the strategies you'll use to maximize your returns.

2. Choose a broker

After determining your goals, the next step is to choose a broker that offers options trading. Look for a broker that is reputable, licensed, and has a strong track record in options trading. Consider the fees the broker charges, the trading platform it offers, and any other factors that are important to you.

3. Complete the account application

Once you've chosen a broker, the next step is to complete the account application. This will typically involve providing personal information, such as your name, address, and Social Security number, as well as information about your financial situation and investment experience. Be sure to read the application carefully and provide accurate information.

4. Fund your account

After your account has been approved, the next step is to fund it. Most brokers will require a minimum deposit to open an options trading account, which can range from a few hundred dollars to several thousand. You can fund your account via wire transfer, check, or electronic transfer from your bank account.

5. Learn the basics of options

Before you start trading options, it's important to have a solid understanding of the basics. Options trading can be complex, so take the time to learn about the different types of options, how they work, and the risks involved. Your broker may offer educational resources, such as videos or webinars, to help you get started.

6. Choose your options trades

After you've learned the basics of options trading, it's time to choose your trades. There are a variety of strategies you can use, depending on your goals and risk tolerance. For example, you might use a covered call strategy to generate income, or a protective put strategy to hedge against risk.

7. Place your trades

Once you've chosen your trades, it's time to place them. Options trading involves buying and selling contracts, which give you the right to buy or sell an underlying asset at a certain price. Be sure to carefully review the terms of each contract before placing your trade.

8. Monitor your trades

After placing your trades, it's important to monitor them regularly. Options prices can fluctuate quickly, so be prepared to adjust your trades if necessary. Keep an eye out for news or events that could affect the price of the underlying asset, and be ready to act accordingly.

Setting up an options trading account can be a straightforward process, but it's important to take the time to choose the right broker, learn the basics, and carefully choose your trades. By following these steps, you can start trading options with confidence and potentially achieve your investment goals.

Chapter 22: Choosing an Options Broker

Investing in stock options can be a lucrative venture, but choosing the right options broker is crucial for success. With an increasing number of options brokers available today, it may be difficult to decide which one is the best for you. Your decision can have a significant impact on your profits, so it's important to do your research and understand the fundamentals of an options broker.

First and foremost, you need to determine your trading goals and requirements. What kind of trader are you? Are you a beginner or an experienced investor? Do you prefer a high-risk/high-reward approach or a more conservative investment strategy? Determining what works best for you, will enable you to pick the right options broker.

Another factor to consider is the level of options trading you are interested in. Some brokers, particularly those focused on active traders, offer a range of services like level I and level II options trading, while some might provide only basic options trading capabilities.

Keep in mind that options brokers can charge different fees, commission, and margin rates for their services. Low fees, commission, and margin rates can help you save money, but it's important to understand the services offered and the quality of customer support.

Another factor to consider is the trading platform offered by the broker. It's important to have a trading platform that is easy to use and navigate. Ideally, you want to be able to customize your trading experience based on your needs like alerts, charting, and technical indicators. Moreover, the trading platform should be available on desktop, mobile, and web for your convenience.

Types of Options Brokers

Options brokers can be broadly categorized into three types based on the services they provide - Full-service brokers, Discount brokers, and Robo-advisors.

Full-service brokers offer a range of services including advice, research, and recommendations to make investment decisions. They work with investors to understand their financial goals and create customized strategies to achieve those goals. However, they require higher fees and commissions, making them suitable for high net-worth investors.

Discount brokers, on the other hand, provide a basic platform for trading, charging lower fees and commission. With a discount broker, you may be on your own with research tools but no recommendations.

Robo-advisors, as the name suggests, are automated and provide customized portfolios for investors based on their preferences and goals. Robo-advisors can be ideal for beginners who are just starting out with options trading.

Tips for Selecting an Options Broker

1. Research and Comparison

Once you've determined your trading goals and requirements, it's time to do some research on the various options brokers. Take the time to compare the services offered by each broker. You must choose an options broker that meets your needs. Online broker review sites and comparison tools that allow you to compare brokerage fees and features are helpful.

2. Platform and Tools

Options trading requires up-to-date market information and trading tools. A robust platform is essential for executing your strategies, monitoring investments, and getting the necessary alerts in real-time. Technical indicators and charting tools are an essential component in selecting a broker, especially for active traders.

3. Minimum Balance and Fees

Some brokers have no minimum account balance requirements, while others do. Take a look at the minimum account balance requirement and other associated fees before selecting a broker.

Brokers with high account minimums and fees may not be ideal if you're just starting out or have a limited budget.

4. Customer Service

Good customer service is crucial, especially when it comes to trading. You want a broker that provides excellent customer service and support whenever you need it. Look for brokers that offer 24/7 customer service via phone, email, or live chat.

5. Security and Regulation

Investing requires trust, but with online trading, you also need to consider security and regulations. Choose a broker that is regulated by a reputable financial body like the Securities and Exchange Commission (SEC) and/or the Financial Industry Regulatory Authority (FINRA). Broker security is critical, and top brokers use strict security protocols for your protection.

Choosing an options broker is a crucial decision, and it's important to do your research and compare all options available. All brokers are not created equally, and you may want to trade with one that meets your requirements and priorities. Factors such as account balance requirements, fees, trading platform, and customer service can all differ between brokers. Selecting an options broker that is a good match for your needs can ensure that you have a profitable trading experience.

Chapter 23: Understanding Implied Volatility

If you are an options trader or an investor in the stock market, then you have probably heard the term "implied volatility" being thrown around. But what exactly is implied volatility, and why is it so important to traders and investors? In this chapter, we will dig deep into the concept of implied volatility and explore how it affects options pricing and trading strategies.

What is Implied Volatility?

At its core, the concept of implied volatility relates to the perceived risk or uncertainty associated with a particular financial instrument. In the context of options trading, implied volatility refers to the expected future volatility of the underlying asset based on the current market prices of the options.

To put it simply, implied volatility is a measure of the expected magnitude of price swings in the underlying asset over a given period. High implied volatility implies that the market expects significant price movements in the future, while low implied volatility indicates a more stable price environment.

One of the key points to note about implied volatility is that it is an estimation that is derived from current options market prices. Market participants, such as traders and investors, use past trading data and other statistical models to estimate future market volatility.

Why is Implied Volatility Important?

The concept of implied volatility is crucial to options traders and investors because it directly affects the pricing of options contracts. The higher the implied volatility of an option, the more expensive the option will be, as the higher implied volatility implies a greater likelihood of the option moving in-the-money. On the other hand, low implied volatility means that the option is less likely to move in-the-money, and hence it will be cheaper.

Understanding implied volatility is also essential because it can provide insight into market sentiment and expectations. For instance, if the implied volatility of an option is increasing, it could imply that the market is becoming more uncertain or that there is an upcoming event that could cause significant price movements. As such, traders can use implied volatility data as a way to gauge market sentiment and make informed trading decisions.

Calculating Implied Volatility

Calculating implied volatility can be a complicated process, but there are various tools and techniques available to make the process more accessible. One of the most common methods for calculating implied volatility is the Black-Scholes model, which is used to price European-style options.

The Black-Scholes model is based on several key assumptions, such as a constant risk-free rate, no dividend payments, and normally distributed stock price movements. Using the model, traders can input current market prices for an option and other financial data to calculate the implied volatility of the underlying asset.

However, it is worth noting that the Black-Scholes model has its limitations and may not always provide an accurate estimate of implied volatility. Other models, such as the Binomial model and Monte Carlo simulation, can be used to estimate implied volatility and may be more appropriate for certain financial instruments or market conditions.

Interpreting Implied Volatility

Interpreting implied volatility data can be a challenge, even for experienced traders and investors. One of the key factors to consider when interpreting implied volatility is the historical volatility of the underlying asset. If the implied volatility of an option is significantly higher than the historical volatility of the asset, it could imply that the market is overestimating future price movements.
Similarly, if the implied volatility of an option is significantly lower than the historical volatility, it could indicate that the market is underestimating future price movements. As such, traders and investors should always compare implied volatility against historical volatility to gain a more realistic understanding of market expectations.

Another important consideration when interpreting implied volatility is the time horizon of the underlying asset. Implied volatility tends to be higher for options with more extended expiry periods as there is more time for significant price movements to occur. Traders should always take into account the expiry date of the option when interpreting implied volatility data and adjust their trading strategies accordingly.

Trading Strategies for Implied Volatility

Once you have gained a good understanding of implied volatility and its impact on options pricing and market sentiment, you can start developing trading strategies that take implied volatility into account. One popular strategy is known as the "Straddle" strategy. A Straddle is an options trading strategy that involves buying both a call option and a put option with the same strike price and expiry date. The reasoning behind this strategy is that it can be profitable if the underlying asset makes a significant price movement in either direction.

The Straddle strategy is particularly attractive when implied volatility is high, as it implies that the market is expecting significant price movements in either direction. As such, traders can purchase a Straddle to profit from any significant price movements while limiting their risk exposure.

Another strategy that traders can use when implied volatility is high is to sell options contracts. The high implied volatility means that options premiums will be more expensive, and traders can take advantage of this by selling options contracts and collecting premiums. However, this strategy comes with higher risk as implied volatility can increase further, causing significant losses. As such, it is essential to manage risk and always have an exit strategy in place when selling options contracts.

Implied volatility is a crucial concept in options trading and investing, and gaining a good understanding of it is essential for success in the financial markets. It is a measure of the expected future volatility of the underlying asset based on current market prices and can provide insight into market sentiment and expectations. Calculating implied volatility can be challenging, but there are various techniques and models available to make the process more accessible.

Interpreting implied volatility data requires consideration of historical volatility and time horizons, and traders can develop trading strategies that take implied volatility into account. The Straddle strategy and selling options contracts are two popular strategies that traders can use when implied volatility is high. Regardless of the trading strategy, it is essential to manage risk and always have an exit strategy in place.

In summary, understanding implied volatility is an essential tool for any trader or investor looking to navigate the complex world of the financial markets. By taking the time to develop a strong understanding of this concept, you can gain new insights, make more informed trading decisions, and ultimately increase your chances of success.

Chapter 24: Understanding Historical Volatility

Investing in the financial markets always involves an element of risk. Understanding the level of risk associated with any given asset is crucial for any investor to make informed decisions. Volatility is one of the key metrics used by investors to determine the level of risk associated with an asset. Volatility refers to the degree of variation in the price of an asset over a certain period, and it can be measured using different methods, including historical volatility.

Historical volatility is a measure of the past price fluctuations of a security. It is calculated based on the standard deviation of the returns over a given period. In other words, historical volatility measures how much the price of an asset has deviated from the mean or average price over a certain period. The higher the historical volatility of an asset, the more likely it is to experience large price swings in the future.

Historical volatility is an essential metric for investors as it provides a basis for forecasting future price movements. By knowing the historical volatility of an asset, investors can estimate the likelihood of future price changes, set risk-management strategies, and adjust their portfolios according to their risk tolerance levels.

Calculating Historical Volatility

Historical volatility can be calculated using different techniques, including the standard deviation method and the average true range method.

The standard deviation method is the most popular way to calculate historical volatility. It involves looking at the past returns of an asset and calculating the standard deviation of these returns over a specific period. The standard deviation represents the dispersion of returns around the average return. The larger the standard deviation, the higher the historical volatility of an asset.

The formula for calculating historical volatility using the standard deviation method is as follows:

$$HV = SD \times \sqrt{(n)}$$

Where HV is historical volatility, SD is the standard deviation of returns, and n is the number of periods used to calculate the standard deviation.

For example, suppose we want to calculate the historical volatility of a stock over the past 30 days. We first calculate the daily returns of the stock over the past 30 days. We then calculate the standard deviation of these daily returns, which we assume to be 2.5%. Finally, we use the formula above to calculate the historical volatility as follows:

$$HV = 2.5\% \times \sqrt{(30)} = 43.30\%$$

The historical volatility of the stock over the past 30 days is 43.30%.

The average true range method is another way to calculate historical volatility. This method measures the average range between the high and low price of an asset over a given period. This range is adjusted to account for gaps in the price, which can distort the range calculation. The average true range is then multiplied by a factor to provide a measure of historical volatility. The factor used depends on the investor's preference and experience with the asset.

Interpreting Historical Volatility

Investors use historical volatility to determine the level of risk associated with an asset. The higher the historical volatility of an asset, the riskier it is considered to be. High historical volatility implies that the asset is prone to large price swings, which could result in substantial gains or losses for investors.

On the other hand, low historical volatility suggests that the asset is stable, with little fluctuation in its price. Such assets are generally less risky but may offer lower returns.

Investors can use historical volatility to set risk-management strategies that match their risk tolerance level. For example, an investor with a high-risk tolerance may be comfortable investing in an asset with high historical volatility, knowing that any price increase will result in significant profits. On the other hand, an investor with a low-risk tolerance may prefer to invest in an asset with low historical volatility, even if it means lower returns.

Limitations of Historical Volatility

While historical volatility is an essential measure of risk, it has some limitations that investors should be aware of. Historical volatility only provides information on past price movements and may not necessarily predict future volatility accurately. As such, investors should complement historical volatility with other metrics that provide a more comprehensive picture of the asset's risk.

Moreover, historical volatility assumes that price movements are symmetrical and that the gains and losses are equally likely. However, this may not be the case in reality, where price movements may be skewed towards one direction. In such cases, investors may need to adjust the historical volatility calculation to account for this asymmetry in price movements.

Finally, historical volatility does not take into account external factors that may influence an asset's price movements. These factors may include economic indicators, political events, or company-specific news, among others. As such, investors should combine historical volatility with other fundamental and technical analysis to make informed investment decisions.

Historical volatility is a crucial metric that measures the past price movements of an asset. It is one of the key indicators used by investors to determine the risk associated with an asset and provides a basis for forecasting future price movements. However, investors should keep in mind the limitations of historical volatility and complement it with other metrics to make informed investment decisions. By understanding historical volatility and its role in investment decisions, investors can make more informed choices and manage their risks more effectively.

Chapter 25: Using Technical Analysis in Options Trading

Technical analysis is an essential tool for successful options trading. It involves studying past performance through charts and indicators to identify trends that indicate future market movements. Technical analysis in options trading enables traders to make informed decisions about market direction, timing, and entry and exit points for their trades.

Options traders use technical analysis to analyze a wide range of data, including price and volume trends, momentum indicators, support and resistance levels, and other market indicators such as relative strength index (RSI), moving averages, and moving average convergence divergence (MACD).

Price and Volume Trends

Price and volume trends analysis is a significant aspect of technical analysis in options trading. Traders use price and volume trends by studying changes in the market price and trading volumes of a particular security. Common tools used to study price trends include candlestick charts, line charts, and bar charts.

Candlestick charts are the most widely used price and volume trend indicators in technical analysis. They represent the price movement of a security over a given time interval, such as a day, a week, or a month. Candlestick charts are used to show the opening price, the closing price, the highest price, and the lowest price within a specified period. Traders use the candlestick chart to identify patterns that indicate potential market movements.

Momentum Indicators

Momentum indicators are technical indicators that traders use to understand the speed or strength of price movement in a particular security. Traders use momentum indicators to understand market trends with the aim of predicting future movements.

The relative strength index (RSI) is a widely used momentum indicator that measures the strength of a security's price action by comparing the average gains and losses over a specified period. RSI ranges from 0 to 100, with readings above 70 indicating overbought conditions and readings below 30 indicating oversold conditions.

Another popular momentum indicator is the moving average convergence divergence (MACD). It is used to identify changes in a security's momentum, strength, direction, and duration. The MACD works by comparing the difference between two moving averages of closing prices. Traders use the lines' crossover and divergence points to identify potential trading opportunities.

Support and Resistance Levels

Another vital aspect of technical analysis in options trading is understanding support and resistance levels. Support levels are the price areas where traders anticipate a high demand for a security, which is expected to stop or "support" the price from dropping further. Resistance levels, on the other hand, are price levels where traders anticipate a decrease in demand for a stock and may sell, which results in the security's price decrease.

Traders use technical analysis to identify the support and resistance level and use that information to execute trades. For instance, a trader might place a buy trade near a support level in anticipation that the stock's value will rise from the level. Conversely, a trader may place a sell trade near a resistance level, assuming that the stock's value may decrease.

Moving Averages

Moving averages, which are calculated as an average of a security's closing prices over a specified time interval, can help traders identify trends, momentum, and support and resistance levels. Two of the most common moving averages are the Simple Moving Average (SMA) and the Exponential Moving Average (EMA).

The SMA is a straightforward average of a security's closing price over a specific period. For instance, a trader might use a 10-day SMA to measure the average closing price of a security for the past ten days. In contrast, the EMA places more emphasis on recent prices, typically within the last few days.

Traders use moving averages to identify support and resistance levels. For instance, a trader might use a 50-day SMA to identify the long-term trend of a security. If the current market price is above the 50-day SMA, it might indicate a bullish market and vice versa.

Technical analysis in options trading is a critical tool that traders use to study price and volume trends, momentum indicators, support and resistance levels, and moving averages to identify potential market opportunities. Traders use technical analysis to predict future market movements and execute trades. Technical analysis requires patience, discipline, and a scholarly approach to studying the market's past performance to identify patterns and trends that may indicate future movements.

As an options trader, it is essential to remember that technical analysis is not foolproof. The market is volatile, and past performance may not necessarily indicate future movement. Therefore, traders need to use other market analysis tools, including fundamental analysis, news, and market sentiment, to make informed trading decisions.

Chapter 26: Using Fundamental Analysis in Options Trading

The world of options trading is a complex and dynamic ecosystem, with a variety of different strategies and approaches available to traders. However, one of the most important tools in any trader's arsenal is fundamental analysis, which involves analyzing an underlying asset's financial and economic data to determine its overall value and potential for growth or decline. By using fundamental analysis in options trading, traders can make more informed decisions about which options to buy or sell, and when to do so.

To understand how fundamental analysis can be used in options trading, it's important to first understand the basics of options themselves. At its most basic level, an option is a contract that gives the holder the right, but not the obligation, to buy or sell an underlying asset at a specific price (known as the strike price) on or before a certain date (known as the expiration date). Options can be used for a variety of purposes, including hedging, speculation, and income generation.

But how do traders decide which options to buy or sell, and at what price? This is where fundamental analysis comes in. By analyzing the financial and economic data related to the underlying asset, traders can make informed decisions about its true value and potential for growth or decline. This information can then be used to determine the strike price and expiration date of the options being traded.

There are a number of different factors that can be considered when performing fundamental analysis in options trading. These include:

- Financial metrics: Traders can analyze the underlying company's financial statements, such as its balance sheet, income statement, and cash flow statement, to get a sense of its overall financial health and performance. Key metrics to look at might include revenue growth, profit margins, return on equity (ROE), and debt levels.

- Industry trends: Traders can also look at broader industry trends to get a sense of how the underlying company is positioned relative to its competitors. This might include trends in revenue growth, market share, or technological advancements.

- Macroeconomic factors: Traders should also consider broader macroeconomic factors that might impact the underlying company's performance. This might include factors such as interest rates, inflation, and overall economic growth.

By considering these and other factors, traders can develop a more detailed understanding of the underlying asset and its potential for growth or decline. This, in turn, can help inform their options trading decisions.

So how might this play out in practice? Let's look at a hypothetical example. Say you're considering buying call options on a particular stock. Before doing so, you might perform a fundamental analysis of the underlying company to determine its overall financial health and prospects for growth. Based on this analysis, you might conclude that the company is undervalued relative to its competitors and has strong prospects for future growth.

You might then use this information to inform your options trading strategy. For example, you might choose a strike price and expiration date that reflects your expectations for the stock's future performance. If you believe that the stock is likely to rise in the near term, you might choose a strike price that is slightly higher than the current market price. If you believe that the stock will continue to perform well over a longer period of time, you might choose a longer expiration date to give the stock more time to appreciate.

Of course, there are no guarantees when it comes to options trading, and even the most careful fundamental analysis can't predict the future with 100% accuracy. However, by using fundamental analysis in options trading, traders can make more informed decisions about which options to buy and sell, and can increase their chances of success over the long term.

It's worth noting that fundamental analysis is just one of many tools and strategies available to options traders. Other strategies might involve technical analysis, market sentiment analysis, or a combination of different approaches. Ultimately, the key to successful options trading is to develop a strategy that works for your individual goals and risk tolerance, and to continually refine and adjust that strategy based on changing market conditions.

Fundamental analysis is a vital tool for options traders looking to make informed decisions about which options to buy and sell, and when to do so. By analyzing the financial and economic data related to the underlying asset, traders can gain a deeper understanding of its value and potential for growth or decline, and can use this information to inform their options trading decisions. While there are no guarantees in options trading, fundamental analysis can help increase the chances of success over the long term.

Chapter 27: Trading Options on Earnings

Trading Options on Earnings

Options trading is one of the most popular ways to invest in the stock market. It offers investors a variety of trading strategies to make money, including the ability to trade options on earnings. Trading options on earnings is a popular strategy for traders looking to profit from the volatility that often follows a company's quarterly earnings report.

In this chapter, we will discuss how options work, how to trade options on earnings, and some strategies for success.

What Are Options?

Options are financial instruments that give buyers the right, but not the obligation, to buy or sell an underlying asset such as a stock, ETF, or index, at a predetermined price and date. There are two main types of options: call options and put options.

A call option gives you the right to buy a stock at a specific price, known as the strike price, at or before the expiration date. A put option, on the other hand, gives you the right to sell a stock at the strike price at or before the expiration date.

Options allow traders to control a large amount of stock with a small amount of money, which is known as leverage. Options also offer investors a hedge against market volatility since they can limit losses by buying put options or reduce the cost of buying stocks by selling call options.

Trading Options on Earnings

Earnings season is a great time to trade options because it often results in volatility. When a company reports earnings, the market reacts to the news, and the stock price can either increase or decrease rapidly.

There are a few options trading strategies that traders use to take advantage of earnings reports.

Straddle

One options trading strategy is the straddle. A straddle is when a trader buys both a call option and a put option at the same strike price, giving them the right to buy or sell the stock at the same price. This strategy can be a bit expensive since it requires buying two options, but it can be effective if the stock price moves significantly in either direction.

For example, suppose a trader buys a straddle on a company that reports earnings. They buy a call option and a put option with a strike price of $100 each. If the stock price goes up to $120, the call option will be in-the-money, and the trader can sell the option for a profit. If the stock price goes down to $80, the put option will be in-the-money, and the trader can sell the option for a profit.

Strangle

Another options trading strategy is the strangle. A strangle is similar to a straddle but uses different strike prices. In a strangle, the trader buys a call option and a put option with different strike prices, but the expiration date is the same. This strategy can be cheaper than a straddle, but it requires a larger price move to become profitable.

For example, suppose a trader buys a strangle on a company that reports earnings. They buy a call option with a strike price of $110 and a put option with a strike price of $90. If the stock price goes up to $120, the call option will be in-the-money, and the trader can sell the option for a profit. If the stock price goes down to $80, the put option will be in-the-money, and the trader can sell the option for a profit.

Iron Butterfly

The Iron Butterfly is an advanced options trading strategy that can be used during earnings season. This strategy involves selling both a call option and a put option, but at different strike prices. The trader also buys a call option and a put option at the same strike price as the sold options.

This strategy can minimize the cost of trade, but also limit potential profit.

For example, suppose a trader sells a call option with a strike price of $100, a put option with a strike price of $90, and also buys a call option and a put option with a strike price of $95 each. If the stock price stays between $90 and $100, the trader can profit from the premiums received. If the stock price goes above $100 or below $90, the trader can still make a profit if the price moves significantly and the premium is greater than the cost of buying the options.

Risks of Trading Options on Earnings

As with any investment, trading options on earnings does involve risks. The biggest risk is that the stock price may not move in the direction that the trader anticipates. If the stock price doesn't move significantly, the trader may lose money on the options that expire worthless. The risk is even higher if the trader buys multiple options, such as in a straddle or a strangle.

Another risk of trading options on earnings is that the trader may buy a call option or a put option that expires before the earnings report is released. In this case, the trader may lose their investment if the stock price doesn't move significantly after the earnings report comes out.

Trading options on earnings is a popular strategy among traders looking to profit from the volatility that often follows a company's quarterly earnings report. Options allow traders to control a large amount of stock with a small amount of money, which is known as leverage. Options also offer investors a hedge against market volatility since they can limit losses by buying put options or reduce the cost of buying stocks by selling call options.

There are a few options trading strategies that traders use to take advantage of earnings reports, such as the straddle, the strangle, and the Iron Butterfly. As with any investment, trading options on earnings does involve risks, such as the risk that the stock price may not move in the direction that the trader anticipates. It is important to research the company and plan a trading strategy before investing in options on earnings.

Chapter 28: Options Trading Tax Implications

Options trading has been a popular investment strategy for many investors due to its potential for profit and hedging potential. However, while it can be lucrative, options trading can also be complex and challenging to understand, especially regarding tax implications. Tax implications can have a significant impact on an investor's profits, so it is essential to be informed about the tax rules and regulations surrounding options trading. In this chapter, we will discuss the basics of options trading, how taxes work with options trading, and what you need to know to stay compliant with the Internal Revenue Service (IRS) rules.

Understanding Options Trading

Options trading is a type of financial derivative that involves buying and selling options contracts. These contracts give the owner the right, but not the obligation, to buy or sell an underlying asset, such as a stock, at a predetermined price (also known as the strike price) on or before a specified date (also known as the expiration date).

Call options are options contracts that give the owner the right to buy an underlying asset at the strike price, while put options give the owner the right to sell an underlying asset at the strike price. Options trading can be used for a variety of investment strategies, including hedging, speculation, and income generation.

Taxation of Options Trading

The taxation of options trading depends on the type of option being traded, the holding period, as well as the investor's tax status. The two primary categories of options are:

1. Non-equity options - These are options contracts that do not involve shares of stock, such as index options and options on futures. Non-equity options are taxed as Section 1256 contracts by the IRS.

2. Equity options - These are options contracts that involve shares of stock. Equity options are taxed slightly differently by the IRS than non-equity options.

The holding period for options trading also affects how the profits from options are taxed. The holding period is the time between the purchase and sale of an option. If an option is held for less than one year, it is considered a short-term capital gain or loss, while options held for more than one year are considered long-term capital gains or losses.

Short-term capital gains are taxed at the investor's ordinary income tax rate. In contrast, long-term capital gains are generally taxed at a lower tax rate than short-term capital gains. Long-term capital gains are taxed at either 0%, 15%, or 20%, depending on the investor's income bracket.

Taxation of Non-Equity Options

As previously mentioned, non-equity options are taxed as Section 1256 contracts by the IRS. Section 1256 contracts are generally marked-to-market at the end of the year. This means that any marked-to-market gain or loss is realized as if the contract was sold and repurchased at year-end. Marked-to-market gains/losses are taxed at the investor's ordinary income tax rate, regardless of their holding period.

If an investor has a net loss from their Section 1256 contracts at the end of the year, this loss can be carried back up to three years and forward up to five years to offset other taxable income.

Taxation of Equity Options

Equity options are taxed differently than non-equity options. When an equity option is exercised, and the stock is sold, the option seller is treated as selling stock in the open market at the time of the option's exercise. This means that the profit or loss on the option's sale is taxed as a short-term or long-term capital gain or loss, depending on the holding period.

When an investor sells an equity option before the expiration date, the profit or loss is taxed as either a short-term or long-term capital gain or loss, depending on the holding period.

Assignment of Options

The assignment of an option occurs when the option buyer exercises their right to buy or sell the underlying asset at the strike price. When this happens, the option seller is obligated to fulfill the contract by delivering the underlying asset.

If an option is assigned, the tax implications differ depending on whether the option was a call or a put:

1. Call options - If a call option is assigned, the option seller will be required to sell the underlying asset at the strike price. The profit or loss on the sale is taxed as a short-term or long-term capital gain or loss, depending on the holding period.

2. Put options - If a put option is assigned, the option seller will be required to buy the underlying asset at the strike price. The cost of the purchase is added to the option's premium, and the profit or loss on the sale is taxed as a short-term or long-term capital gain or loss, depending on the holding period.

Options trading can be a lucrative investment strategy for those who understand and follow the rules of the trade. Understanding the tax implications of options trading is essential for any investor. The taxation of options trading depends on the type of option being traded, the holding period, and the investor's tax status. To ensure compliance with the IRS regulations, investors should consult a tax professional with experience in options trading to help with tax planning and reporting.

Chapter 29: Exercising Options

An option is a financial contract that gives the holder the right, but not the obligation, to buy or sell a particular asset or security at a specified price within a certain time frame. For instance, if you hold an option to buy 100 shares of XYZ company at $50 per share within the next three months, you have the option to exercise it, or to let it expire, based on the prevailing market conditions.

Exercising an option involves making a decision to either buy or sell the underlying asset at the agreed upon price, known as the strike price. The process of exercising options can be complex and depends on several factors such as the market price of the asset, the expiration date, and the time value of money. In this chapter, we will explore the basics of exercising options and how it works.

Types of Options

Before we delve into the process of exercising options, it is essential to understand the different types of options available to investors. Options come in two fundamental types: call options and put options. A call option gives the holder the right to purchase an underlying asset at a fixed price, whereas a put option gives the holder the right to sell an underlying asset at a fixed price.

When an investor buys a call option, they are betting that the price of the underlying asset will rise above the strike price before the option's expiration date. If the price does rise, the option will be exercised, and the investor can purchase the asset at the agreed-upon strike price and then sell it for a profit in the open market. If the market price of the asset remains below the strike price until the expiration date, the option will expire worthless, and the investor will lose their investment.

When an investor buys a put option, they are betting that the price of the underlying asset will fall below the strike price before the option expires. If the price falls, the option will be exercised, and the investor can sell the asset at the agreed-upon strike price, regardless of the lower market price. If the market price of the underlying asset remains above the strike price until the expiration date, the option will expire worthless, and the investor will lose their investment.

Exercising Call Options

The process of exercising a call option is relatively straightforward. If an investor holds a call option, they have the right to buy the underlying asset at the agreed-upon price until the expiration date. They only need to pay the strike price and take possession of the asset. The investor's decision to exercise the option will depend on the prevailing market price of the underlying asset.

For example, if an investor holds a call option for 100 shares of XYZ company at $50 per share and the market price of the stock rises to $60 per share, they stand to make a $10 per share profit. If the investor decides to exercise the option, they will buy the shares at the agreed-upon price of $50 per share and immediately sell them on the open market for $60 per share. The profit per share would be $10, and the total profit would be $1,000 (100 shares x $10 per share).

However, not all investors decide to exercise their call options. If the market price of the underlying asset remains below the strike price, it would not make sense to exercise the option. In such scenarios, investors choose to let the option expire worthless or sell it back to the market before the expiration date.

Exercising Put Options

The process of exercising a put option is slightly different from that of a call option. Rather than buying the underlying asset at the agreed-upon price, the holder of a put option has the right to sell the underlying asset at the agreed-upon price until the expiration date. If the market price of the asset drops below the strike price, the investor can sell the asset at the higher strike price and make a profit.

For instance, suppose an investor holds a put option for 100 shares of ABC company at $40 per share and the market price of the stock falls to $30 per share. In this case, if the investor decides to exercise the option, they can sell the shares for $40 per share, making a profit of $10 per share or $1,000 overall. If the market price of the underlying asset remains higher than the strike price until the expiration date, it would not make sense to exercise the option. In such cases, the investor could let the option expire worthless or sell it back to the market before the expiration date.

Factors Affecting Exercise of Options

Exercising options is not always a straightforward process, and several factors influence an investor's decision to exercise or not to exercise their options. The most significant factor that affects the exercise of options is the market price of the underlying asset. If the market price of the underlying asset is equal to or higher than the strike price, an investor may choose to exercise their call option or allow it to expire worthless. Similarly, if the market price of the underlying asset is equal to or lower than the strike price, an investor may choose to exercise their put option or let it expire worthless.

Another factor affecting the exercise of options is the time left until the expiration date. As the expiration date approaches, the time value of the option decreases, and the investor may choose to exercise it instead of waiting. Suppose an investor holds a call option for 100 shares of XYZ company, with an agreement to buy them at $50 per share within the next three months. Suppose that the market price of the stock has risen to $55 per share and that the expiration date is two weeks away. In this scenario, the investor may decide to exercise the option immediately to avoid the risk of losing their profit if the market price falls below $50 per share again.

The volatility of the underlying asset's market price is another factor affecting the exercise of options. The more volatile an asset's value is, the greater the risk for the investor. As a result, investors may choose to exercise their options sooner to avoid the possibility of losing their investment. For example, if an investor holds a call option for a technology stock that announces a significant drop in revenue, the investor may choose to exercise the option before the market price drops too much.

Exercising options is an essential aspect of options trading, and investors must understand how it works. Buying call or put options involves making a decision on whether to exercise the option when the market price of the underlying asset reaches the agreed-upon price. Investors prefer to exercise call options when the market price of the underlying asset rises above the strike price, and the preference to exercise put options is when the market price of the underlying asset falls below the strike price. The process of exercising options is affected by several factors, such as the market price of the underlying asset, the time left until the expiration date, and the volatility of the asset's price. Investors need to weigh these factors to make an informed decision on when to exercise their options.

Chapter 30: Options Assignment

When it comes to options trading, there are a variety of different strategies and techniques that investors use to try and maximize their returns and minimize their risks. One of the most important concepts to understand when it comes to trading options is the idea of options assignment. In this chapter, we'll take an in-depth look at what options assignment is, why it happens, and what the risks and benefits of options assignment can be for investors.

What is Options Assignment?

At its core, options assignment is the process by which an option seller (also known as the option writer) is forced to sell (in the case of a call option) or buy (in the case of a put option) the underlying asset at the strike price once the option is reached its expiration date. This can happen either if the buyer of the option exercises their right to buy or sell the underlying asset, or if the option is assigned to another investor.

Essentially, options assignment happens when an option seller has written an option, and either the buyer decides to utilize their option to purchase the underlying asset, or the option seller's broker assigns the option to another investor who is willing to exercise their option. It's important to note that options sellers cannot control whether or not an option is assigned, and therefore this risk should be factored into any options trading strategy.

Why Does Options Assignment Happen?

The primary reason why options assignment happens is due to the fact that options contracts are contracts that give one party (the buyer) the right to buy or sell an underlying asset at a specific price, while the other party (the seller) takes on the obligation to deliver or accept delivery of that underlying asset at that same price. This obligation is often referred to as the "counterparty risk" of options trading.

When a buyer exercises their right to buy or sell the underlying asset, the seller (or writer) of the option is obligated to fulfill that transaction. If the option is in the money (meaning that the price of the asset has moved in favor of the buyer), then it becomes beneficial for the buyer to exercise their option and purchase or sell the underlying asset at the strike price. In this case, the option writer would be assigned to fulfill that order, regardless of their personal preference.

In some cases, options can also be assigned by brokers or firms based on their own internal requirements. This is often the case when options positions are being cleared or regulated by exchanges, and is less common than options being assigned by a buyer exercising their option.

What are the Risks of Options Assignment?

For option writers, the risks of options assignment can be significant.
If the underlying asset has moved significantly in the buyer's favor,
then the option seller may be forced to sell the asset at a price below
market value, resulting in a loss. Additionally, if the option seller was
not planning on selling the asset (either because they were hoping
for the option to expire worthless or because they did not hold the
underlying asset), then they may be forced to make a purchase of the
asset in order to fulfill the option.

Furthermore, options assignment can also result in unexpected tax
liabilities for option sellers. Because they are obligated to sell the
asset at the strike price, regardless of market value, options sellers
may be forced to sell the asset at a loss in order to fulfill the option.
This can result in an unwanted tax hit if they have to sell at a loss.

What are the Benefits of Options Assignment?

For options buyers, the benefits of options assignment are clear. By
exercising their right to buy or sell the underlying asset, they can
lock in a profit or minimize their losses if the price of the asset
moves in their favor. Additionally, being assigned an option means
that the buyer can take ownership of the underlying asset, which can
be beneficial if they were hoping to hold the asset for a longer period
of time.

For options sellers, the benefits of options assignment can be more nuanced. While there are certainly risks involved, options sellers can use options assignment as a way to generate income or mitigate risk in their portfolios. By writing options contracts, they can receive premiums upfront for taking on the obligation to sell or buy the underlying asset. Additionally, by using options as part of a wider hedging strategy, they can mitigate risk by setting the terms of their obligation in advance.

Options Assignment in Action

To better understand how options assignment works in practice, let's take a look at a simplified example.

Suppose that an investor writes a call option with a strike price of $50 for a stock that is currently trading at $45. The investor receives a premium of $1 per share ($100 total) from the buyer of the option.

If the stock price stays below $50, then the option will expire worthless, and the option seller gets to keep the premium. However, if the stock price rises above $50 (even if it's just by a few cents), then the buyer of the option may exercise their right to buy the stock at $50 per share, forcing the option seller to sell the stock at that price.

If the stock price rises to $55, then this would result in a loss for the option seller, since they would be forced to sell the stock at $50, resulting in a net loss of $5 per share. However, if the option seller was not holding the underlying asset in their portfolio, then they would also have to purchase the stock in order to fulfill the option. This could result in a total loss of $10 per share ($5 net loss for selling the stock + $5 purchase price for buying the stock).

On the other hand, if the option seller had already purchased the stock in their portfolio, then they could fulfill the option by selling the shares they already owned at the strike price of $50. In this case, they would still make a profit from the sale (since they had purchased the shares at a lower price), but their profit would be capped at $5 per share.

Options assignment is a key concept in options trading, and understanding its risks and benefits is essential for anyone looking to use options as part of their investment strategy. While options buyers benefit from being able to lock in profits or minimize losses, options sellers must be aware of the potential downsides, such as being forced to sell or buy an asset at an unfavorable price. By incorporating options into a wider portfolio management strategy, investors can balance these risks and benefits to help maximize their returns.

Chapter 31: Options Spreads and Combination Strategies

Options Spreads and Combination Strategies

Options trading can be a tricky proposition for those who are not familiar with its intricacies. However, there are ways to reduce risk while still being able to reap the benefits of the market. One of the most popular methods is through the use of options spreads and combination strategies.

In this chapter, we will explore the basics of options spreads and combination strategies, discuss the different types of strategies available, and provide some examples of how they can be used in various market scenarios.

What are Options Spreads and Combination Strategies?

In order to fully understand options spreads and combination strategies, it is necessary to first define what an option is. An option is a contract between two parties that gives the buyer the right, but not the obligation, to buy or sell an underlying asset (usually stocks) at a predetermined price (strike price) on or before a specific date (expiration date).

Options spreads involve buying and selling multiple option contracts at the same time in order to achieve a specific goal, such as reducing risk or increasing profits. Combination strategies, on the other hand, are similar to spreads but involve the use of different types of options (such as calls and puts) in order to gain an advantage in the market.

Types of Options Spreads

There are several different types of options spreads, each with its own unique characteristics and risk-reward ratios. Some of the most common spreads include the following:

1. Bull Call Spread - This is a bullish strategy in which the trader buys a call option at a lower strike price and sells a call option at a higher strike price. The maximum profit is achieved if the price of the underlying asset goes up, while the maximum loss is limited to the initial cost of the options.

2. Bear Put Spread - This is a bearish strategy in which the trader buys a put option at a higher strike price and sells a put option at a lower strike price. The maximum profit is achieved if the price of the underlying asset goes down, while the maximum loss is limited to the initial cost of the options.

3. Iron Butterfly - This is a neutral strategy in which the trader sells both a call and a put option at the same strike price and buys a call and a put option at a higher and lower strike price, respectively. The maximum profit is achieved if the price of the underlying asset

remains near the strike price, while the maximum loss is limited to the initial cost of the options.

4. Calendar Spread - This is a non-directional strategy in which the trader buys a longer-term option and sells a shorter-term option at the same strike price. The maximum profit is achieved if the price of the underlying asset is near the strike price at the expiration of the shorter-term option, while the maximum loss is limited to the initial cost of the options.

Types of Combination Strategies

There are also several different types of combination strategies, which involve the use of both calls and puts in order to achieve a specific goal. Some of the most common strategies include the following:

1. Straddle - This is a non-directional strategy in which the trader buys both a call and a put option at the same strike price. The maximum profit is achieved if the price of the underlying asset moves significantly in either direction, while the maximum loss is limited to the initial cost of the options.

2. Strangle - This is a non-directional strategy in which the trader buys both a call and a put option at different strike prices. The maximum profit is achieved if the price of the underlying asset moves significantly in either direction, while the maximum loss is

limited to the initial cost of the options.

3. Butterfly - This is a directional strategy in which the trader buys one call option at a lower strike price, sells two call options at a higher strike price, and buys one call option at an even higher strike price. The maximum profit is achieved if the price of the underlying asset is near the middle strike price at expiration, while the maximum loss is limited to the initial cost of the options.

4. Condor - This is a directional strategy in which the trader buys one call option at a lower strike price, sells one call option at a slightly higher strike price, sells one put option at an even higher strike price, and buys one put option at an even higher strike price. The maximum profit is achieved if the price of the underlying asset remains within a specific range at expiration, while the maximum loss is limited to the initial cost of the options.

Examples of Options Spreads and Combination Strategies

Let's take a look at a few examples of how these different options spreads and combination strategies can be used in various market scenarios.

Example 1: Bull Call Spread

Suppose a trader believes that XYZ stock is going to increase in price over the next few months. The trader decides to use a bull call spread strategy by buying a call option at a lower strike price of $50 and selling a call option at a higher strike price of $55. The trader pays $2 for the $50 call option and sells the $55 call option for $1. The net cost of the strategy is $1.

If the price of XYZ stock goes up to $60 at expiration, the trader will receive $10 from the $50 call option ($60 - $50) and will have to pay out $5 for the $55 call option ($60 - $55). The total profit will be $4 ($10 - $5 - $1), which is a 400% return on investment.

If the price of XYZ stock stays below $50 at expiration, the trader will lose the entire $1 net cost of the strategy.

Example 2: Strangle

Suppose a trader believes that the price of ABC stock is going to move significantly in either direction over the next few weeks. The trader decides to use a strangle strategy by buying a call option at a strike price of $50 and buying a put option at a strike price of $45. The trader pays $2 for the call option and $1 for the put option, for a total net cost of $3.

If the price of ABC stock goes up to $60 at expiration, the trader will receive $10 from the call option ($60 - $50) and will lose the $1 net cost of the put option. The total profit will be $6 ($10 - $1 - $3), which is a 200% return on investment.

If the price of ABC stock goes down to $40 at expiration, the trader will receive $5 from the put option ($45 - $40) and will lose the $2 net cost of the call option. The total profit will be $3 ($5 - $2 - $3), which is a 100% return on investment.

If the price of ABC stock stays between $50 and $45 at expiration, the trader will lose the entire $3 net cost of the strategy.

Options spreads and combination strategies are useful tools for reducing risk and increasing profits in the options market. However, it is important to understand the different types of spreads and strategies available, as well as the potential risks and rewards of each. By using these strategies wisely and with proper planning, traders can effectively navigate the complex world of options trading and achieve success in the market.

Chapter 32: Writing Covered Calls

There are many ways to invest in the stock market, but few strategies offer the level of flexibility, stability, and risk control as writing covered calls. Writing covered calls is an options trading strategy that involves two main steps: buying or holding a stock and selling a call option on that stock. The goal is to generate income and/or protect your stock holdings from downside risks.

In this chapter, we will explore the basics of writing covered calls, the benefits and risks, how to choose the right stocks, and how to customize the strategy to fit your investment goals and risk tolerance.

Chapter 1: The Basics of Writing Covered Calls

First, let's define some key terms. A call option is a contract that gives the buyer the right but not the obligation to buy a specific stock at a specific price (strike price) by a specific date (expiration date). The seller of the call option (the writer) receives a premium (income) from the buyer and is obligated to sell the stock if the buyer exercises the option. A covered call is a call option that is sold on a stock that the seller already owns or buys at the same time of selling the call option. By doing so, the seller of the covered call holds a "covered" position and is not exposed to unlimited risk, as in naked call writing.

How does writing covered calls work? Let's say you own 100 shares of XYZ stock, which is currently trading at $50 per share. You may sell a call option on those shares, say, a call option with a $55 strike price and a three-month expiration date. You receive a premium of, let's say, $2 per share, or $200 in total (multiplying the premium per share by the number of shares, 100). If the stock price remains below $55, the option expires worthless, and you keep the premium, which is a 4% return on your investment ($200 divided by $5,000, the cost of 100 shares at $50 each). If the stock price rises above $55 and the buyer of the option exercises it, you have to sell your shares for $55, which is a 10% return ($5,500 divided by $5,000), plus the premium you received, which reduces your effective selling price to $53 ($55 minus $2). If the stock price rises above $57, your gain is capped at $7 per share ($5,700 from selling the shares for $57 minus $5,000 cost of the shares), and you may miss out on further appreciation.

The benefits of writing covered calls are clear: you can generate income from your stock holdings, hedge against downside risks, and limit your upside potential. However, there are also risks and limitations to consider.

The Benefits and Risks of Writing Covered Calls

Generating income: Writing covered calls can be a reliable source of income, especially in volatile or sideways markets, where stocks may not appreciate much but still offer high volatility or strong fundamentals. The premiums you receive from selling call options can boost your overall return, provide liquidity, and help you cover your selling costs. Moreover, you can choose the strike price and expiration date that suits your objectives and expectations, and adjust your strategy accordingly. For example, if you want to generate more income, you may sell call options with a closer expiration date, higher strike price, or riskier stocks. If you want to protect your downside risk, you may sell call options with a lower strike price, longer expiration date, or more stable stocks.

Hedging against risks: Writing covered calls can also protect your stock holdings against downside risks, such as market corrections, earnings misses, or geopolitical events. By selling call options, you create a cushion of income that offsets some of the losses you may face if the stock price drops. For example, if you own 100 shares of XYZ stock at $50 per share and sell a call option with a $55 strike price and a three-month expiration date for a $2 premium, your break-even price is $48 ($50 minus $2). If the stock price falls below $48, you still have a cushion of $200 ($2 per share), which reduces your loss. If the stock price stays above $48, you keep the premium and may sell another call option to generate more income, hedge further risks, or sell the stock entirely.

Limiting your upside potential: The downside of writing covered calls is that it limits your upside potential, especially in strongly trending or volatile markets. If the stock price rises above the strike price of the call option you sold, you have to sell the stock, even if you think it may go higher. Thus, you may miss out on some gains, or your effective selling price may be lower than the market price. For example, if you sell a call option on XYZ stock with a $55 strike price and the stock price rises to $60, you have to sell the stock for $55, which means you miss out on $5 per share. Moreover, if you sell a call option with a low premium, you may end up with a low effective selling price, as the premium may not offset all the gains you could have made. Therefore, it is essential to sell call options with a careful balance of strike price, expiration date, and premium, and to adjust your strategy according to market conditions and your investment goals.

Choosing the Right Stocks for Writing Covered Calls

What stocks are suitable for writing covered calls? Ideally, you want to choose stocks that have some or all of the following characteristics:

- Strong fundamentals: Stocks that have high earnings, revenue, or dividend growth, low debt-to-equity ratios, high margins, or other metrics that show stable or improving performance. The idea is to invest in stocks that are likely to appreciate or at least maintain their value, and to have a good cushion against market downturns.

- High volatility: Stocks that have volatile prices, either due to their industry, size, competition, or other factors. The goal is to sell call options that have high premiums, which are more likely to be assigned, to generate more income or hedge against downside risks.

However, high volatility stocks also have higher risk, as their prices may swing wildly, and the premiums may not always offset the losses.

- Stagnant or declining stocks: Stocks that have low or negative price momentum, or that trade in narrow ranges for extended periods. The idea is to sell call options that have lower strike prices, which are less likely to be assigned, to generate income or gain from slight price appreciation. The risk is that these stocks may not appreciate much, and the premiums may not offset the losses if the stock price drops.

- Stocks with low correlations: Stocks that have low correlations with each other, or with other assets such as bonds, commodities, or currencies. The goal is to diversify your portfolio and reduce your overall risk by choosing stocks that behave differently under different market conditions. However, low correlation also means lower predictability and lower return potential.

When choosing stocks for writing covered calls, it is important to do your research, analyze the fundamentals and the technicals, and keep an eye on the news and events that may affect the stock price. You may also want to use screening tools or services that filter stocks based on predefined criteria, such as volatility, earnings growth, or dividend yield. Ultimately, the key is to choose stocks that fit your investment goals, risk tolerance, and overall portfolio strategy.

Customizing Your Covered Call Strategy

Writing covered calls is not a one-size-fits-all strategy. Every investor has different objectives, expectations, and constraints, and should customize their strategy accordingly. Here are some ways to customize your covered call strategy:

- Varying the strike price and the expiration date: Depending on your outlook for the stock price and the market, you may choose different strike prices and expiration dates for your call options. For example, if you expect the stock price to rise moderately, you may sell call options with a higher strike price and a longer expiration date. If you expect the stock price to drop, you may sell call options with a lower strike price and a shorter expiration date. Moreover, you may roll over or close your call options before the expiration date if you want to capture gains or avoid losses.

- Hedging with put options: Writing covered calls can be combined with buying put options to create a protective collar or a synthetic covered call. A put option is a contract that gives the buyer the right but not the obligation to sell a specific stock at a specific price (strike price) by a specific date (expiration date). By buying put options that have a lower strike price than the covered call options you sold, you can protect your downside risk, as the put options will offset some of the losses if the stock price drops below the strike price. However, buying put options also reduces your income potential and may increase your overall cost.

- Using technical indicators and charts: Writing covered calls can benefit from using technical analysis, which uses charts and indicators to identify trends and patterns in stock prices. Technical analysis can help you choose the right strike price, expiration date, and premium based on historical price data and market trends. However, technical analysis also has limitations and may not always be accurate or reliable.

- Diversifying with other strategies: Writing covered calls can be combined with other options trading strategies or other asset classes, such as bonds, real estate, or commodities. By diversifying your portfolio, you can reduce your overall risk and increase your income potential. For example, you may use a covered call ladder, which involves selling call options with different strike prices and expiration dates to create a constant income stream and to capture gains from moderate stock price movements. Or, you may use a covered call ETF, which invests in a basket of stocks and sells covered calls on those stocks to generate income.

Writing covered calls is a versatile and effective strategy for generating income and hedging against risks in the stock market. By selling call options on stocks you own or buy, you can create a cushion of income that offsets some of the losses if the stock price drops, while still benefiting from moderate gains. Moreover, you can customize your strategy according to your investment goals, risk tolerance, and market outlook, by varying the strike price, expiration date, and premium, or by combining other options trading strategies or asset classes. However, writing covered calls also has limitations and risks, such as limiting your upside potential, relying on market conditions, and subjecting you to losses if the stock price drops significantly. Therefore, it is important to do your due diligence, analyze your portfolio, and choose the right stocks and strategy that fit your needs.

Chapter 33: Selling Cash-Secured Puts

If you're an investor looking to generate some income or add to an existing position without necessarily buying more shares of a stock, selling cash-secured puts might be an option worth considering. Put options give buyers the right to sell an underlying asset at a specified price on or before a specified date. As the seller of a put option, you collect a premium for assuming the obligation to buy the underlying asset at the specified price, known as the strike price, if the buyer exercises their option.

Selling puts can be a way to earn income if you expect the underlying stock to remain relatively stable or increase in value during the life of the option. This strategy can also be used to enter a position at a lower price than the current market price, or to add to an existing position at a lower cost basis. However, selling puts also entails risk, as you could be obligated to buy the underlying stock at the strike price if the stock's price falls below the strike price.

To mitigate this risk, selling cash-secured puts is a popular strategy. This means that you have enough cash on hand to buy the underlying stock at the strike price if you are assigned the option. In other words, you only sell puts on stocks that you would be comfortable owning at the strike price. By securing the cash, which is typically held in a margin account, you can avoid having to buy the underlying stock with borrowed funds, which can add additional risk.

An example of a cash-secured put trade might look like this: suppose you want to buy 100 shares of XYZ stock, which is currently trading at $50 per share. You could sell a put option with a strike price of $45, expiring in one month, for a premium of $100. If the stock price remains above $45 by the expiration date, you keep the premium and the option expires worthless. If the stock price falls below $45 and the option is exercised, you are obligated to buy the 100 shares of XYZ stock for $45 per share, which would cost you $4500. However, since you have secured the cash in your account, you don't need to use borrowed funds or face a margin call.

Benefits of Selling Cash-Secured Puts

One of the main benefits of selling cash-secured puts is the ability to generate income. By selling puts on stocks that you would like to own at a lower cost basis, you can earn a premium for assuming the obligation to buy those stocks at a specific price. This income can be used to supplement other investments or to reinvest in additional stocks or options. In general, the higher the volatility of the underlying stock or index, the higher the premium you can collect for selling puts.

Another benefit of selling cash-secured puts is the ability to enter or add to a position at a lower cost basis. If you are bullish on a stock or index, but you feel that the current price is too high, you can sell puts with a strike price below the current market price. If the stock price falls below the strike price, you can buy the stock at a discount and potentially profit if the price recovers. This can be a way to add to an existing position at a lower cost basis or to enter a new position without having to buy at the current market price.

Selling cash-secured puts can also be a way to manage risk. By securing the cash for the trade, you can avoid using borrowed funds or facing a margin call if the option is exercised. This can reduce the potential for losses in a falling market. Additionally, by only selling puts on stocks that you would be comfortable owning at the strike price, you can limit your downside risk.

Risks of Selling Cash-Secured Puts

Like any investment strategy, there are risks associated with selling cash-secured puts. The main risk is the potential for the stock price to fall below the strike price, resulting in the obligation to buy the stock at a higher price than the market price. In this scenario, you would be forced to buy the stock at the higher strike price even though the market price is lower, resulting in a loss. This risk is greater in volatile markets or with stocks that are particularly risky or have a history of being highly volatile.

Another risk of selling cash-secured puts is opportunity cost. If the stock price remains above the strike price and the option expires worthless, you collect the premium but miss out on potential gains in the stock price. This can be frustrating if you were bullish on the stock and it ends up performing well, but you didn't own it or only owned a smaller position.

Finally, there is the risk of missing out on potential gains if the stock price rises quickly. If the stock price rises above the strike price before the option expires, the buyer of the option will not exercise their right to sell the stock at the lower price, and you will keep the premium but miss out on any gains in the stock price. This risk can be mitigated by choosing strike prices that are close to the current market price, but it is still a risk to consider.

Selling cash-secured puts can be a useful strategy for investors looking to generate income, enter or add to a position at a lower cost basis, or potentially manage risk. By only selling puts on stocks that you would be comfortable owning at the strike price, you can limit some of the downside risk, while securing the cash can help prevent you from using borrowed funds or facing margin calls. However, there are risks involved, including the potential for losses if the stock price falls below the strike price and the opportunity cost of missing out on potential gains. As with any investment strategy, it is important to consider the risks and benefits carefully before deciding if it is right for you.

Chapter 34: Using Protective Puts

As investors, we all know that risks are an integral part of investing in financial markets. We can make informed decisions based on our analysis and research, but we cannot predict the future with accuracy. Fluctuations in markets and various macroeconomic factors can affect the value of our investments. This uncertainty can be unnerving for some investors, especially those who have invested a significant amount of money in the market.

To tackle this inherent risk, investors have resorted to different hedging strategies, with protective puts being one of the most popular methods. Protective puts provide a safety net for investors by mitigating potential losses. In this chapter, we will discuss what protective puts are, how they work, and when and how to use them.

Understanding Protective Puts

A protective put is a financial instrument that hedges an investor's exposure to losses in their stock position. Put options provide the holder with the right, but not the obligation, to sell an underlying asset (in this case, the stock) at a predetermined price (the strike price) until a specified expiration date. In simpler terms, a put option acts as insurance for the stock. If the price of the stock falls below the strike price, the holder of the put option can sell the stock at the strike price, thereby limiting their losses.

For example, assume an investor holds 100 shares of ABC Company, currently trading at $50 per share. The investor can purchase a put option at a strike price of $45 for a premium of $2 per share. By doing so, the investor is protected from any losses below $45 per share until the expiration date of the option. If the price of the stock falls to $40 per share, the investor can exercise the put option, sell the shares at $45 per share, and limit their loss to $300 ($5 per share x 100 shares).

The Benefits of Protective Puts

The primary benefit of using protective puts is downside protection. They are an excellent tool for investors who are bullish on a stock but are concerned about short-term market fluctuations. Protective puts allow investors to maintain exposure to the potential upside of the stock while limiting potential losses.

Protective puts can also be used in combination with other investment strategies, such as covered calls, to enhance returns and lower risks. Covered calls are a popular strategy where investors sell call options on stocks they already own, thereby generating income from the premium received. By adding protective puts to the mix, investors can protect their downside risk in case the stock price falls.

Another benefit of protective puts is that they allow investors to maintain a long-term investment horizon. Many investors get jittery during periods of market volatility and tend to sell their positions at the slightest hint of a downturn. Protective puts provide a cushion to this knee-jerk reaction and allow investors to stay invested for the long haul.

Evaluating the Cost of Protective Puts

While protective puts provide downside protection, they come at a cost. The premium paid for the put option reduces the returns from the underlying stock. Hence, investors need to evaluate if the cost of the put option is justified based on the potential downside risk.

One effective method to evaluate the cost of a protective put is to calculate the break-even point. The break-even point is the point at which the cost of the put option is equal to the potential loss from the stock. For example, if an investor holds 100 shares of XYZ Company, currently trading at $100 per share, and purchases a put option at a strike price of $95 for a premium of $2 per share, the break-even point would be $93 per share ($95 – $2 premium). This means that if the stock falls below $93 per share, the investor would start making a profit on their put option, offsetting some or all of their losses from the stock.

Therefore, before purchasing a protective put option, investors need to assess the potential downside risk and the cost of the put option. The cost of the put option should be proportional to the downside risk, and the breakeven point should be realistic.

When to Use Protective Puts

Protective puts are an excellent hedging tool for investors who are bullish on a stock but want to limit their downside risk. They are especially beneficial when markets are volatile, and the potential downside risk is higher than usual. Investors can also use protective puts to protect their portfolio against events such as company-specific news, earnings announcements, or geopolitical events that may affect stock prices negatively.

However, protective puts are not suitable for all investors. They are typically more popular among experienced investors who have a thorough understanding of options and how they work. Novice investors may find them challenging to use and may end up increasing their risks instead of mitigating them. Additionally, protective puts are not a guarantee against losses. Markets and stocks can behave unpredictably, and protective puts may become ineffective in extreme scenarios.

How to Implement Protective Puts

While purchasing protective puts may seem easy, they require a certain amount of strategy, as they need to be timed correctly to be effective. Here are some essential steps to implement protective puts effectively:

1. Analyze the stock's current price trends to determine if it is likely

to go lower in the future.

2. Choose an expiry date and a strike price for the put option slowly. Ideally, the expiry date should be after any significant news or earnings announcements, and the strike price should be below the current stock price.

3. Calculate the cost of the protective put and determine the break-even point.

4. Purchase the put option and maintain it until it expires or the stock price sufficiently rises.

5. If the stock price reaches the strike price, consider selling the put option or exercising it to sell the stock at the strike price.

Protective puts are a great tool for investors looking to protect their stocks against downside risk. They provide the peace of mind of knowing that losses are limited while maintaining exposure to the potential upside of the stock. However, they are not suitable for all investors, and inexperienced investors may find it challenging to use them. Additionally, they come with a cost, and investors need to evaluate the put's cost against the potential downside risk of the stock. Investors should remember that protective puts are not a guarantee against losses, and even with them, markets and stocks can behave unpredictably.

Chapter 35: Creating a Collar Strategy

Whenever investors desire to protect their equity's downside risk while still being able to participate in any potential upside, they frequently use a collar strategy. It is a well-known solution in financial markets that provides an effective method for hedging against a decline in the price of a security or portfolio while still keeping some upside potential.

To understand the collar strategy, it is necessary first to understand a few fundamental concepts of options trading. Options are contracts that provide the buyer with the right but not the obligation to purchase or sell the underlying asset at a specific price within a set time frame. The buyer of the option is referred to as a holder or owner. Still, it is usually used in conjunction with the seller, who is referred to as the writer or seller.

The price of an option, or its value, comprises two key components: intrinsic value and time value. Intrinsic value is a measure of the worth of a stock that could be obtained if the option holder exercised the option and sold the underlying stock instantly, while time value is the premium that the holder pays to hold the option for a certain time frame.

In the collar strategy, investors use the options market to produce a safeguarded range of outcomes that protects against unlimited downside risk and offers some upside potential. Typically, the investor holds a long position in the underlying equity asset and purchases a protective put option while simultaneously selling a covered call option. The protective put option helps in mitigating the investor's equity risk by offering a minimum price at which the equity can be sold, while the covered call option provides additional income from the underlying asset's appreciation, which is capped.

To create a collar strategy, investors must follow several steps.

Step 1: Identify the underlying asset

The first and most crucial step in creating a collar strategy is to determine which underlying asset to use. This could be a stock, index, exchange-traded fund (ETF), or mutual fund.

Step 2: Identify the number of shares held

Once the underlying asset has been identified, the number of shares held should be determined.

Step 3: Determine the strike price for the put option

The strike price of the protective put option determines the minimum sale price for the underlying asset. It is essential to note that the put option must be in the money when the trade is executed.

Step 4: Determine the expiration date for the options

The expiration date for the options sets the length of time that the collar strategy will be in effect. It is essential to choose an expiration date that aligns with the investor's investment objectives.

Step 5: Identify the price for the call option

The price for the covered call option is determined by the investor. It is a premium that the investor receives for selling the option.

Step 6: Determine the number of call options to sell

The number of call options sold is determined by the number of shares held by the investor. In general, the number of call options sold should be equal to the number of shares held by the investor.

Step 7: Implement the collar strategy

The final step in creating a collar strategy is to implement it. The investor buys the put option, sells the call option, and holds the underlying asset.

An example of a collar strategy is as follows:

Suppose an investor holds 1,000 shares of XYZ stock, which is currently trading at $50 per share. The investor wants to protect against a decline in the stock's price while still being able to participate in any potential upside. To create a collar strategy, the investor could buy a protective put option with a strike price of $45, which is currently priced at $2 per share, and sell a covered call option with a strike price of $60, which is priced at $1.5 per share.

If the price of XYZ stock falls below $45, the investor can exercise the put option and sell the stock at $45, thereby limiting the downside. If the price of XYZ stock rises above $60, the investor has limited the potential upside, as the call option seller must sell the underlying asset at $60.

However, the investor will have still made a profit on the sale of the call option, which will have helped offset some of the losses from the decline in the stock price.

Overall, the advantages of putting a collar on your equity positions consist of more limited losses than would happen if ownership was held uncovered. Notwithstanding the price of the underlying assets, the hedge guarantees that the downside risk is confined, and the investor is free from worrying about large losses. Additionally, it can also provide protection against market volatility, reducing the risk of adverse market moves. The disadvantages include the opportunity costs of capping the upside, as well as the complexity of managing several options positions.

The collar strategy is a useful tool for investors looking to hedge their equity exposure while still participating in some potential upside. By buying a protective put option and selling a covered call option, the investor creates a safeguarded range of outcomes that protects against unlimited downside risk while offering some upside potential. As the strategy can be complex to manage, investors should consult with their financial advisors to determine if a collar strategy is appropriate for their investment objectives, risk tolerance, and trading experience.

Chapter 36: Trading Index Options

In the world of modern finance, a wide range of investment vehicles offer traders opportunities to manage risk and generate profits. One notable example is index options, which represent contracts giving the holder the right (but not the obligation) to buy or sell a basket of stocks that tracks a specific market index.

Compared to traditional stock options or other derivatives, index options offer a number of potential advantages. For one, they provide greater portfolio diversification, as investors can access entire market sectors or regions with a single trade. Additionally, index options are typically more liquid and offer lower transaction costs than individual stock options, making them an attractive choice for traders who seek efficient and reliable securities.

In this chapter, we'll explore the basics of trading index options, including how they work, their key features and characteristics, and some practical strategies for maximizing returns and managing risk in complex market conditions.

Overview of Index Options

Before we dive into the specifics of index options trading, let's first define what an index is. An index is a group of listed equities that represent a particular market sector, country, or region. The most widely-known U.S. index is the S&P 500, which includes 500 of the largest publicly-traded companies in the U.S.

So what are index options? An index option contract allows the buyer the right (but not the obligation) to trade an amount of stocks that track a particular index at a fixed price at any given time. For example, if a trader wants to bet that the S&P 500 will increase, they can purchase a call option contract. Conversely, if they think the S&P 500 will decrease, they can purchase a put option contract.

The price of an index option is determined through a pricing model based on a combination of multiple factors, such as the index value, the strike price agreed at purchase, time remaining until expiration, and implied volatility.

This complexity is why index options are primarily used by sophisticated investors and traders, as they require a higher level of knowledge and risk management than traditional stock or mutual fund trading.

Advantages of Index Options

Index options may offer several benefits over traditional investment vehicles:

1. Portfolio Diversification: Index options allow traders to access entire market sectors or geographic regions with a single trade, providing a more diversified portfolio.

2. Cost Efficiency: Compared with individual stock options, index options tend to have lower minimum investment requirements, making them more accessible for traders seeking to manage their risk exposure.

3. Liquidity: Index options are more widely traded than individual stock options, providing greater liquidity (i.e., the ability to enter and exit trades with ease) and lower transaction costs.

4. Centralized Market: Since index options are regulated and traded through established exchanges, traders are more likely to benefit from standard pricing and transparent trading practices.

5. Hedging: Traders with existing positions in stocks or mutual funds can use index options to hedge their exposure to specific market factors, helping to limit overall risk exposure.

Types of Index Options

There are two types of index options:

1. Call options: A call option allows the holder to buy a specific index at a pre-agreed price before a certain date.

2. Put options: A put option allows the holder to sell a specific index at a pre-agreed price before a certain date.

Like traditional stock options, index options come with both European-style (exercise date is the last day of trading) and American-style (exercise date can take place at any time before expiration) options.

The mechanics of index options are similar to traditional options trading. Buyers pay a premium to purchase the option, with the amount depending on the strike price and time remaining until expiration. The option becomes profitable if the index moves in the expected direction (up for calls, down for puts) with the amount of profit determined by the time remaining until expiration.

Index Options Trading Strategies

Now that you have a basic understanding of index options, let's explore some common trading strategies that can help traders maximize profits and manage risk exposure.

1. Covered Calls: A covered call strategy involves buying stock and simultaneously selling an equivalent number of call options. The goal is to slightly reduce the cost of stock ownership while collecting the premium value of options.

As long as the stock price remains stable or rises slightly, this strategy can result in a steady stream of income for the trader. However, if the stock price drops significantly, the investor is still at risk of substantial losses.

2. Protective Puts: Protective puts are another common way to hedge against downside risk. Essentially, you buy a put option at a strike price that represents the level at which you are willing to sell your stock.

If the stock price drops significantly, the option becomes profitable--and can offset the losses of the stock. There is a premium to pay for these options, but the increased security can often be worth it.

3. Long Call (or Put) Strategy: The Long Call (or Put) strategy is the most straightforward approach to trading index options. It involves purchasing call (or put) options contracts for an index that the trader believes will rise (or fall).

If the index price rises above the contract's strike price before it expires, the investor can sell it for a profit. If the index price falls below the contract's strike price, the trader takes a loss. This strategy is particularly useful if you believe a significant price swing is imminent.

4. Calendar Spread: The calendar spread (also called horizontal spread) strategy involves selecting two options contracts with the same strike price but different expiration dates. The trader buys the option with the longer expiration date and sells the option with the shorter expiration date. This strategy allows traders to benefit from the difference in premium due to the longer time remaining until expiration for the purchased option.

5. Iron Condor: The Iron Condor is a multi-legged options strategy that consists of four options contracts: two near-the-money covered calls and two near-the-money puts. This strategy protects against a modest price movement in either direction and allows traders to collect income from the options premiums if the index remains stable.

6. Straddle: The Straddle strategy involves simultaneously purchasing a call and a put at the same strike price and expiration date. This approach is useful if you expect significant volatility, as it allows profits to be made in both directions.

Final Thoughts on Index Options Trading

Index options trading offers traders a wide range of opportunities to generate profits and hedge against market risks. However, it requires significant knowledge, experience, and risk management skills to succeed.

Before trading index options, it is essential to carefully evaluate your financial goals and risk tolerance and to develop a clear trading strategy that aligns with your objectives. By leveraging the diverse range of trading strategies available to you and implementing strong risk management practices, you can unlock the full potential of index options trading and position yourself for long-term success in the dynamic world of modern finance.

Chapter 37: Trading Options on Futures

Futures contracts are a form of derivatives used by investors to hedge against the potential fluctuations of underlying assets such as commodities, currencies, and indices. Options on futures, on the other hand, provide traders with the opportunity to speculate on the direction of futures markets without the obligation to buy or sell the underlying asset.

Options on futures can be used for a variety of purposes, ranging from hedging against potential losses to taking advantage of market volatility for profit. In this chapter, we will explore the basics of trading options on futures, including their key characteristics, pricing models, and trading strategies.

Key Characteristics of Options on Futures

Options on futures have several distinct features that differentiate them from other financial instruments. Some of the important characteristics that traders should understand include:

1. Underlying Asset: An option on futures contract gives the holder the right, but not the obligation, to buy or sell a futures contract at a predetermined price (strike price) on or before a specific date (expiration date). The underlying asset of an options contract is the futures contract, which represents an agreement to buy or sell an underlying asset at a future date.

2. Exercise Style: Options on futures contracts can be either American or European style. American-style options can be exercised at any time before the expiration date, while European-style options can only be exercised on the expiration date.

3. Premium: Options on futures have a premium, which is the price that the buyer pays and the seller receives for the right to buy or sell the underlying futures contract. The premium is determined by various factors such as the current market price of the futures contract, the strike price, the time left until expiration, and the volatility of the underlying asset.

4. Volume and Open Interest: The volume of an options contract refers to the number of contracts traded on a particular day, while open interest is the total number of outstanding contracts at any given time. High volume and open interest indicate active market participation and liquidity, which are important for traders to enter and exit positions easily.

5. Margin Requirements: Options on futures contracts also have margin requirements, which refer to the amount of cash or collateral that traders must maintain in their trading accounts to support their positions. Margin requirements depend on factors such as the current market price of the futures contract, the strike price, and the volatility of the underlying asset.

Pricing Models for Options on Futures

The pricing of options on futures is based on various mathematical models, including the Black-Scholes model, binomial model, and Monte Carlo simulation. These models use inputs such as the current market price of the underlying futures contract, the strike price, the time left until expiration, and the volatility of the underlying asset to estimate the fair value or theoretical price of the option.

In general, options with lower strike prices and longer expiration periods tend to have higher premiums because they have a higher probability of being profitable. Options that are far out of the money (i.e., the underlying futures contract is far away from the strike price) tend to have lower premiums because they have a lower probability of being profitable.

Trading Strategies for Options on Futures

Options on futures can be used in a variety of trading strategies, including directional bets, hedging, and income generation. Some of the common trading strategies that traders can use with options on futures include:

1. Long Call: A long call option strategy involves buying a call option on a futures contract with the expectation that the underlying asset will increase in price. If the futures price rises above the strike price by expiration, the trader can exercise the option and buy the futures

contract at a lower price, realizing a profit. If the futures price does not rise above the strike price, the trader will lose their premium.

2. Short Call: A short call option strategy involves selling a call option on a futures contract with the expectation that the underlying asset will not increase in price. If the futures price remains below the strike price by expiration, the trader can keep the premium and realize a profit. If the futures price rises above the strike price, the trader will be obligated to sell the futures contract at a lower price and will incur a loss.

3. Long Put: A long put option strategy involves buying a put option on a futures contract with the expectation that the underlying asset will decrease in price. If the futures price falls below the strike price by expiration, the trader can exercise the option and sell the futures contract at a higher price, realizing a profit. If the futures price does not fall below the strike price, the trader will lose their premium.

4. Short Put: A short put option strategy involves selling a put option on a futures contract with the expectation that the underlying asset will not decrease in price. If the futures price remains above the strike price by expiration, the trader can keep the premium and realize a profit. If the futures price falls below the strike price, the trader will be obligated to buy the futures contract at a higher price and will incur a loss.

5. Spreads: Options spreads involve buying and selling multiple

options on the same or different futures contracts. Spreads can be used to limit risk, reduce margin requirements, and generate income. Some of the common spreads used with options on futures include the bull call spread, bear call spread, bull put spread, and bear put spread.

Options on futures are versatile trading instruments that can be used for speculation, hedging, and income generation. Before trading options on futures, it's important to understand their key characteristics, pricing models, and trading strategies. Options on futures require careful consideration of market conditions, underlying asset volatility, and risk management to be successful.

Chapter 38: Leverage and Margin in Options Trading

Option trading is a popular investment strategy utilized by investors in the financial markets. It enables traders to utilize certain market conditions to rake in profits without owning the underlying asset. The options market offers a wide range of benefits, but one of the most important is leverage. With leverage, traders have the opportunity to make larger profits compared to their initial investment. In this chapter, we will be discussing leverage and margin in options trading, which is critical to becoming a successful options trader.

What is Leverage?

Leverage in options trading refers to the ability of a trader to control a large amount of shares of an underlying asset with minimal investment capital. It is a strategy that creates the potential for gains and losses that are significantly higher than the initial investment. The term "leverage" generally refers to borrowing capital to increase the size of a trade or investment, allowing investors to take on more risk than they would with their available budget. It's important to note that leverage increases the size of potential gains or losses, making it a double-edged sword for traders.

Typically, leverage is achieved through the use of margin. Margin is essentially a loan from a broker which allows traders to increase the size of their trading position, above and beyond their initial investment. For example, if a trader has a $5,000 trading account and wishes to purchase options on a specific stock, a margin account allows the trader to borrow additional funds from their broker to increase the size of their position. The concept of leverage is essential in options trading as it provides traders with the potential to earn significant profits while minimizing initial investment risks.

Types of Leverage in Options Trading

There are three types of leverage utilized in options trading: mechanical leverage, implied leverage, and calendar leverage.

Mechanical leverage

Mechanical leverage refers to the purchase of a call or put option on a stock or other security. The use of call and put options facilitates the mechanical leverage by allowing investors to control the underlying assets or securities with less capital.

For example, if a trader wishes to purchase AAPL at $100 per share with broker's fee of $50, they would need to make a cash investment of $10,050. However, if the same trader chooses to buy 10 call options at the strike price of $100, with a cost of $5 per option, the initial investment would only be $5,050, giving traders effective mechanical leverage. Now, if the price of AAPL increases to $120, then the trader can sell the option for a higher premium of $20, or $20,000 in total capital gain. The trader's profit in this scenario would be \$9,950. In this way, mechanical leverage gives traders the ability to take advantage of market conditions to maximize profits.

Implied leverage

Implied leverage, also known as Delta, refers to the sensitivity of an option's price to changes in the underlying asset's price. For example, a call option with a delta of 0.8 will increase the value of the option by \$0.80 for every \$1 increase in the underlying asset's price. This means that traders can gain implied leverage by choosing call options with higher delta values. The higher the delta, the greater the potential profits.

On the other hand, implied leverage can result in an investor's loss of the entire initial investment. If the underlying asset's price moves against the trader's position, the option can quickly lose its value, leaving the trader with nothing. Therefore, it's important to manage the risks of implied leverage to avoid any harmful effects on the trader's capital.

Calendar leverage

The use of calendar leverage is meant to decrease time decay by using more than one option contract with different expirations. The idea is to sell options with shorter expiration dates and purchase options with longer expiration dates. This method can reduce the impact of time decay and increase the profit potential of traders.

For example, if a trader buys a call option that expires in one year, they can choose to sell a call option that expires in three months. The premium of the shorter call option can contribute to decreasing the cost of the longer call option, decreasing the net debit of the trader's investment. Using calendar leverage requires careful consideration to avoid losing the invested capital, as it relies on correct prediction and timing for a profit.

The Advantages of Leverage in Options Trading

The primary advantage of leverage in options trading is the ability to control a large position utilizing small amounts of capital. Other advantages are:

1. Lowered Costs

Leverage permits traders to execute trades that otherwise would not have been possible due to the high cost of buying or selling an asset. Thus, traders can use a relatively small amount of money to achieve similar results to an investment several times that size.

2. Maximized Profits

Using leverage allows traders to take advantage of market volatility and multiply their profits. In this way, the investment returns can exceed what could be achieved without leverage.

3. Diversification

The use of leverage in options trading gives traders the opportunity to diversify their portfolio to include securities they might not normally be able to invest in without the high costs often associated with them.

The Risks of Leverage in Options Trading

While leverage provides traders with potential higher returns, it also carries significant risks. The leverage ratio merely increases the size of potential profits and losses. This makes it essential for traders to thoroughly understand the markets they're trading in and manage their risks appropriately. Some of the significant risks include:

1. Margin Calls

Margin calls occur when the equity in a trader's account falls below the minimum required by the broker. When this happens, the broker will demand additional funds from the trader to meet the required maintenance margin level. The failure to meet the margin call can lead to the liquidation of all or part of the trader's holdings.

2. Loss of Capital

The use of leverage in options trading also increases the probability of a trader's loss of capital. The high degree of uncertainty inherent in the market calls for careful consideration and management of risks to avoid heavy losses.

3. Hyper-Losses

The use of leverage with options trading can cause a trader to lose more than what was initially invested. The potential for such hyper-loss can cause a cascade of irreversible damage to the trader's account, which can be challenging to recover from.

Option trading is an investment strategy that relies on the use of leverage and margin to control larger positions within the financial market. While leverage provides traders with the potential to achieve higher returns, it also comes with significant risks and losses. Therefore, understanding the intricacies of leverage and margin is essential for any options trader. The wise use of leverage in options trading can be an invaluable tool for maximizing returns, while minimizing losses. The key is to take calculated risks and manage all the risks with a prudent approach.

Chapter 39: Managing an Options Portfolio

Options are financial derivatives that give investors the right, but not the obligation, to buy or sell a security, currency, or index at a predetermined price within a specific time frame. Options can be used for speculative or hedging purposes, depending on the investor's risk appetite and investment objectives. To manage an options portfolio, investors must understand the different types of options, their pricing and valuation, and the strategies to use them effectively.

Types of Options

There are two main types of options, namely call options and put options. A call option gives the holder the right to buy a security, currency, or index at a specified price, known as the strike price, on or before the expiration date. A put option gives the holder the right to sell a security, currency, or index at the strike price on or before the expiration date. Investors can use call options to speculate on price increases, while put options can be used to hedge against price declines.

Options can also be classified as American or European options, depending on when they can be exercised. An American option can be exercised at any time before the expiration date, while a European option can only be exercised on the expiration date. American options typically trade at a premium to European options due to their greater flexibility.

Pricing and Valuation

The pricing of options is determined by various factors, including the asset price, the strike price, the time to expiration, the volatility of the underlying asset, and the risk-free interest rate. The Black-Scholes model is a widely used mathematical formula for pricing options that takes into account these factors.

The Black-Scholes model assumes that the underlying asset follows a lognormal distribution and that investors are risk-neutral. In reality, however, the asset price can be affected by various factors, such as news events, market sentiment, and geopolitical risks. As such, investors must use judgment and experience to adjust the pricing of options based on market conditions.

The valuation of options is also determined by the Greeks, which are sensitivity measures that reflect the impact of various factors on the option price. The five main Greeks are delta, gamma, theta, vega, and rho.

Delta measures the change in the option price relative to a change in the price of the underlying asset. Delta can range from -1 to 1 for call options and from 0 to -1 for put options. Delta is a useful measure of the hedge ratio of an option, as it reflects the degree of exposure to price changes in the underlying asset.

Gamma measures the change in delta relative to a change in the price of the underlying asset. Gamma is highest for at-the-money options and decreases as the option moves in or out of the money. Gamma reflects the degree of exposure to price changes in the underlying asset and can be used to adjust the hedge ratio as the market price changes.

Theta measures the change in the option price relative to a change in time to expiration, assuming other factors remain constant. Theta is negative for all options, as the time decay of options reduces their value over time. Theta reflects the cost of time to an option holder and can be used to adjust the holding period of an option.

Vega measures the change in the option price relative to a change in the volatility of the underlying asset. Vega is highest for at-the-money options and decreases as the option moves in or out of the money. Vega reflects the sensitivity of an option to changes in market volatility and can be used to adjust the portfolio exposure to risk.

Rho measures the change in the option price relative to a change in the risk-free interest rate. Rho is positive for call options and negative for put options, as higher interest rates increase the value of call options and decrease the value of put options. Rho reflects the sensitivity of an option to changes in interest rates and can be used to adjust the hedging costs of an option.

Strategies

There are various strategies that investors can use to manage an options portfolio, depending on their investment objectives and market conditions. Some of the common strategies are as follows:

Covered call: This strategy involves buying a security and selling a call option on the same security at a higher strike price. The premium received from the call option reduces the holding cost of the security and provides income to the investor. However, the investor is exposed to the risk of price appreciation beyond the strike price, as the call option can be exercised by the holder.

Protective put: This strategy involves buying a security and buying a put option on the same security at a lower strike price. The put option provides downside protection to the investor, as it allows them to sell the security at the strike price if the market declines. However, the premium paid for the put option adds to the holding cost of the security and reduces the potential profits.

Straddle: This strategy involves buying a call option and a put option on the same security at the same strike price and expiration date. The straddle benefits from high volatility in the market, as the option that is in-the-money will provide profits that offset the premium paid for the option that is out-of-the-money. However, the straddle can be costly if the market remains stable, as both options will expire worthless.

Spread: This strategy involves buying an option and selling another option on the same security, with different strike prices or expiration dates. The spread reduces the risk exposure of the investor, as the profit from the sold option can offset the loss from the bought option. However, the spread limits the potential profits and increases the transaction costs.

Iron condor: This strategy involves buying a call spread and a put spread on the same security, with different strike prices and expiration dates. The iron condor benefits from low volatility in the market, as the profit from the sold spreads can offset the loss from the bought spreads. However, the iron condor can be risky if the market experiences sudden changes in price or volatility.

Managing an options portfolio requires knowledge, skill, and experience in the financial markets. Investors must understand the different types of options, their pricing and valuation, and the strategies to use them effectively. By using a combination of strategies and adjusting their holdings based on market conditions, investors can manage their options portfolio to achieve their investment objectives while minimizing their risk exposure.

Chapter 40: Interpreting Options Charts

Options trading can be a rather complex and difficult process to understand, especially if you're just starting out. However, options trading can be an excellent way to diversify your portfolio and generate potential profits in both bullish and bearish market conditions.

An option is a financial contract that gives the buyer the right (but not the obligation) to buy or sell an underlying asset at an agreed-upon price (called the "strike price") on or before a specified date (called the "expiration date"). Options can be used to hedge against potential losses or speculate on potential gains. They are generally bought and sold on an options exchange.

One important tool that options traders use to analyze and evaluate their trades is an options chart. An options chart is a graphical representation of an option's price and volatility over time. Options charts can provide traders with important information about the current state of the market, as well as potential trends and opportunities.

In this chapter, we will cover the basics of interpreting options charts, including how to read and analyze different types of charts and indicators.

Types of Options Charts

There are several types of options charts that traders can use to analyze and interpret market trends. Some of the most common types include:

1. Line Charts:

A line chart is one of the simplest types of options charts and is typically used to plot the closing prices of an option over a given period of time. Line charts are useful for identifying overall trends and price movements in the market.

2. Bar Charts:

A bar chart is a more complex type of options chart that shows the open, high, low, and closing prices of an option over a given period of time. Bar charts can provide traders with more detailed information about the range and volatility of an option's prices.

3. Candlestick Charts:

Candlestick charts are similar to bar charts in that they show the open, high, low, and closing prices of an option over a given period of time. However, candlestick charts also provide additional visual cues in the form of "candles." Each candle represents a specific time period and is made up of a "body" (the opening and closing prices) and "wicks" (the highs and lows).

4. Point and Figure Charts:

Point and figure charts are a specialized type of options chart that focuses on the changes in price movements rather than the passage of time. These types of charts use X's and O's to represent price movements and can be useful for identifying potential trends and reversals in the market.

Interpreting Options Chart Patterns

Once you've selected the type of options chart that you want to use, it's important to be able to identify and interpret different chart patterns. Chart patterns can provide traders with insights into potential market trends, potential support and resistance levels, and potential entry and exit points for trades.

Some of the most common types of options chart patterns include:

1. Support and Resistance:

Support and resistance levels are key price levels that an option's price will often bounce off of. Support levels represent areas where buyers are more likely to step in and start buying an option, while resistance levels represent areas where sellers are more likely to start selling an option.

2. Trend Lines:

Trend lines are lines that connect two or more price points on an options chart and can be used to identify potential trends in the market. An uptrend is defined by a series of higher highs and higher lows, while a downtrend is defined by a series of lower highs and lower lows.

3. Head and Shoulders:

Head and shoulders is a common chart pattern that can signal a potential trend reversal in the market. This pattern is characterized by a peak (the "head") between two troughs (the "shoulders"). Traders will often look for a break of the neckline (the support level connecting the two troughs) as a signal to enter a short position.

4. Bullish and Bearish Flags:

Bullish and bearish flags are chart patterns that typically occur after a significant move in an option's price. These patterns are characterized by a short-term consolidation phase (the "flag") that typically resolves in the direction of the original trend.

Using Technical Indicators to Interpret Options Charts

In addition to chart patterns, traders can also use technical indicators to interpret options charts and identify potential trading opportunities. Technical indicators are calculations based on an option's price and volume data that can help traders identify potential trends and market momentum.

Some of the most common technical indicators used in options trading include:

1. Moving Averages:

Moving averages are a simple technical indicator that calculates the average price of an option over a specified period of time. Moving averages can be useful for identifying potential trends and support and resistance levels.

2. Relative Strength Index (RSI):

The RSI is a momentum oscillator that measures the strength and speed of an option's price movements. The RSI is typically used to identify overbought or oversold conditions in the market.

3. Bollinger Bands:

Bollinger Bands are a volatility indicator that uses standard deviation to measure an option's price movements. Bollinger Bands can be useful for identifying potential support and resistance levels and potential breakout points.

4. Moving Average Convergence Divergence (MACD):

The MACD is a trend-following momentum indicator that uses moving averages to identify potential trend changes in the market. The MACD is typically used to identify potential entry and exit points for trades.

Limitations of Options Charts and Technical Indicators

While options charts and technical indicators can be extremely useful tools for identifying potential trading opportunities, it's important to recognize their limitations.
One limitation of options charts is that they can be susceptible to false signals and noise. Trends and patterns in the market can be disrupted by unexpected news events or market volatility, which can make it difficult to rely solely on options charts for decision-making. Similarly, technical indicators can also be susceptible to false signals and noise. Some technical indicators may work better in certain market conditions than others, and it's important to evaluate the effectiveness of a particular technical indicator in relation to current market conditions.

Ultimately, options charts and technical indicators should be used as part of a larger trading strategy and should be evaluated in conjunction with other market data and analysis. By taking a comprehensive approach to trading, traders can increase their chances of success in the options market.

Chapter 41: Evaluating Options with Profit/Loss Diagrams

One of the main challenges in successfully trading options is the ability to comprehend how different strategies will perform under different market conditions. However, if the trader does not have a solid understanding of the potential outcomes of their options strategy, they are exposing themselves to unnecessary risk.

To evaluate these outcomes, we often use profit/loss diagrams. A profit/loss diagram is a graph that evaluates the potential profit or loss of an options strategy at different stock prices. This tool can be tremendously helpful in helping traders visualize, evaluate and compare different options trading strategies.

In this chapter, we will explore how to create and analyze profit/loss diagrams in practical trading scenarios, examine how to use them to determine a strategy's risk and reward, and discuss how to use them to refine our trade decisions.

Constructing Profit/Loss Diagrams

To illustrate how profit/loss diagrams work, let us create an example for a simple options strategy.

Suppose an options trader wants to purchase a call option on a stock that is currently trading at $50 per share. The call option has a strike price of $55 and costs $2 per contract.

To make this investment, the trader will pay $200 ($2 x 100 shares). However, the trader will only profit if the price of the stock rises above the $55 strike price of their call option. In our example, if the stock rises to $60 per share, the trader could sell their share for $60, netting them a profit of $3 per share ($60 - $55). If the trader bought 100 shares worth of contracts, their profit will be $300 ($3 x 100).

The profit/loss diagram for this call option purchase appears in Figure 1.

![]<https://i.imgur.com/rdF9juF.png>

Figure 1: Profit/Loss Diagram for a call option with a strike price of $55 and a premium of $2.

The horizontal line in the middle of Figure 1 represents the options expiration date, where the stock must be trading at a price above the strike price of $55 to return value. To the right of this line, the stock is trading above the strike price, creating a profit. Meanwhile, on the left side of the expiration line, stock prices are too low, resulting in a loss.

The steep line upward on the right of the graph is the profit zone of the options trade. Any stock price higher than the $57 break-even point generates a profit. The final potential profit is unlimited as the stock continues climbing.

In contrast, the steep line pointing downwards indicates the loss zone of the options trade. Any stock falling below the break-even point of $57 will result in a loss in the amount equal to the premium paid for the call option. In this case, the loss is limited to $200. However, if the stock price continues to declines, the loss on the call option will increase.

The break-even point of the call option purchase is when the stock price equals the strike price of the option plus the premium paid ($57 in this example). If the stock price drops below $55, the entire $200 premium paid is transferred to the seller of the call, with the amount of the loss increasing as the stock falls further below the strike price.

Understanding the Break-Even Point

The break-even point is a crucial element of the options trading strategy because it indicates the price at which an investor will have neither a profit nor a loss. Reviewing the graph can help provide the trader with a full view of an options strategy, the potential profit, and various other factors.

In our example, a break-even price of $57, indicates that the stock must exceed that number to initiate a potential profit. The strike price and the premium paid will ultimately determine the break-even point.

Analyzing Profit/Loss Diagrams

The profit/loss diagram can offer investors essential information about the risk and reward levels of a proposed options trading strategy. An understanding of the profit/loss diagram helps the trader comprehend the earnings potential and how the strategy performs at different stock prices.

The two primary aspects a trader should examine are:

1. Maximum Profit
2. Maximum Loss

When building new options strategies, the maximum profit and maximum loss should be examined to quantify whether the anticipated results correlate with the trader's overall objectives.

Maximizing Profit

Examining the profit zone of the profit/loss diagram identifies the maximum profit the strategy can produce. Options strategies seldom have unconstrained upside potential, but some are more fruitful than others.

With a call option, the maximum profit is infinite since there is no limit to how high a stock price can rise. In many cases with the short-term call options, the stock will not significantly move within the timeframe, so there may not be as ample opportunity for profit.

Maximizing Loss

Examining the loss zone of the profit/loss diagram will identify the maximum loss of the strategy. Options strategies should minimize the maximum loss exposure while still being effective in hitting the profit targets.

The premium paid is the maximum loss when buying a call option since the investment will become worthless if the stock price is less than the strike price before the expiration date. In our example above, the maximum loss is $200, which is the premium paid for the call option.

When constructing an option strategy, the trader must face the potential max loss and compare it to the estimated maximum profit to determine whether the risk is tolerable. While option strategies' potential returns can be compelling, the investor must understand the risk and be able to limit the risk exposure to an acceptable level.

Refining Trading Decisions

The profit/loss diagram is an effective tool for refining trading decisions as it provides visual representations of the potential outcomes of different options trading strategies. Helping to identify and understand potential profit and loss zones clarifies how each strategy will function under various scenarios.

Examining the profit/loss diagram can help traders compare options strategies, evaluate their win probabilities, and further analyze the risks and rewards of each option.

Depicts several different possible trading scenarios, each with a different outcome depending on the actual stock price at expiration. Looking at these possible scenarios can help the investor select the best options strategy, given the current market and potential risk exposure.

Option A, is a bullish strategy where the investor expects the stock price to increase. The strategy entails buying a call option with a strike price of $55 and a premium of $2. This strategy warrants an initial investment of $200.

Option B, is a neutral strategy where the investor does not anticipate any significant moves in the stock's price. In this strategy, they sell a call option with a strike price of $60 and a premium of $1, collecting an initial premium of $100.

Option C, is a bearish strategy where the investor expects the stock price to decline. In this strategy, they purchase a put option with a strike price of $45 and a premium of $2, paying an initial investment of $200.

When evaluating the three different options strategies above, we can use the profit/loss diagrams to examine how each strategy will perform in various stock price scenarios.

When the stock is trading at $50 per share at the expiration date, Option A, buying call options, will make the investor lose their entire investment, as the call option is out-of-the-money.

When the stock is trading at $55 per share, Option A would reach break-even, precisely that same value, as this is the strike price plus the premium paid.

If the stock price increases to $60 per share, Option A will reach the maximum profit, resulting in the investor earning a profit of $300 ($3 x 100).

For Option B, the selling party collects the premium of $1 per call option, which equates to $100 for the trade. If the stock price remains below the $60 strike price at the expiration date, Option B will reach its maximum profit.

For Option C, if the stock price is above the $45 strike price at the expiration date, Option C will reach the maximum loss level. If the stock price drops to $40 per share, the investor will earn a profit of

$300 ($3 x 100), which is the maximum profit in this option.

These examples show how profit/loss diagrams help traders and investors in evaluating potential scenarios and refine trading decisions.

Profit/loss diagrams are an essential tool in evaluating the outcomes of various potential options trading strategies. These diagrams provide an easy-to-understand visual representation of how different strategies can react to various market scenarios.

Analyzing profit/loss diagrams helps traders understand the potential maximum profit and maximum loss. This understanding is critical when deciding between different strategies or identifying the risk involved in a particular trade.

When deciding on a strategy, traders must look beyond profit opportunities to examine the associated risks to fully understand the potential outcomes of their investments.

By thoroughly examining a profit/loss diagram, traders can access an exhaustive and unambiguous view of an option's strategy potential outcomes and analyze how each strategy performs under different stock price scenarios. With a solid understanding of the profit/loss diagrams, traders can refine trading decisions and maximize their potential returns while minimizing their maximum loss.

Chapter 42: Using Options for Hedging

Options are contracts that give the holder the right, but not the obligation, to buy or sell an underlying asset at a predetermined price on or before a specified date. The underlying asset could be a stock, a commodity, a currency, or even a futures contract. For investors and traders, options provide a flexible tool for hedging, speculating, and generating income.

Hedging is the practice of reducing or mitigating the risk of adverse price movements in an asset or a portfolio of assets. Hedging is crucial for risk management, especially for those who have exposure to volatile markets or unpredictable events. Hedging can be done using various financial instruments, such as futures, forwards, swaps, and options.

However, options offer distinct advantages over other hedging instruments, such as flexibility, customization, limited risk, and cheaper premiums. Options allow investors to tailor their hedging strategy to their specific needs and risk profile. Options also limit the maximum loss to the premium paid, which can be significantly lower than the margin required for futures or forwards.

Here are some ways investors and traders can use options for hedging:

Protecting a Stock Portfolio

If you own a stock portfolio, you may be concerned about a market downturn that could wipe out a substantial portion of your gains. One way to protect your portfolio is to buy put options on the stocks you own. A put option gives you the right to sell the stock at a specified price, called the strike price, on or before a specified date, called the expiration date.

For example, if you own 100 shares of ABC stock currently trading at $50 per share, you could buy one put option with a strike price of $45 and an expiration date in three months for $2 per share. If the stock price falls below $45, you can exercise the put option and sell the stock at the strike price of $45, limiting your loss to $500 ($50 per share minus $45 per share times 100 shares minus $2 per share premium).

However, if the stock price stays above $45, you can let the put option expire worthless and only lose the premium of $200. In this way, you can protect your stock portfolio from downside risk while still participating in the upside potential.

Using Collars for Downside Protection

Another hedging strategy for stock portfolios is using collars. A collar involves buying a put option and selling a call option at the same time, with the strike prices and expiration dates carefully selected to limit the downside risk and the upside potential.

For example, if you own 100 shares of XYZ stock trading at $60 per share, you could buy a put option with a strike price of $55 and an expiration date in three months for $2 per share, while simultaneously selling a call option with a strike price of $65 and the same expiration date for $1 per share. This collar would limit your downside risk to $500 ($60 per share minus $55 per share times 100 shares minus $2 per share premium), while capping your upside potential at $500 ($65 per share minus $60 per share times 100 shares minus $1 per share premium).

In this way, you can protect your stock portfolio from severe losses while still enjoying some potential gains. However, collars can be more complex and involve higher transaction costs than plain put options.

Hedging a Currency Exposure

If you have a currency exposure, such as an international investment or a business transaction, you may be vulnerable to foreign exchange fluctuations that can affect your profits or losses. To hedge a currency exposure, you can use options to lock in a favorable exchange rate and avoid losses due to unfavorable exchange rate movements.

There are two types of currency options: call options and put options. A call option gives you the right to buy a currency at a specified exchange rate, while a put option gives you the right to sell a currency at a specified exchange rate. You could use these options to hedge your currency exposure depending on whether you expect the exchange rate to rise or fall.

For example, if you are a U.S. company that is importing goods from Japan and expects to pay 100 million yen in six months, but you are worried that the yen might appreciate against the dollar, you could buy a put option on the yen/USD exchange rate to protect yourself from a possible loss. Suppose the current exchange rate is 100 yen/USD, and you buy a put option with a strike price of 95 yen/USD and an expiration date in six months for $0.01 per yen. If in six months, the exchange rate drops to 90 yen/USD due to the yen's appreciation, you can exercise the put option and sell 100 million yen for $1,111,111, effectively locking in a favorable exchange rate of 90 US cents per yen and avoiding a loss of $111,111 compared to the current exchange rate.

However, if the exchange rate stays above 95 yen/USD or appreciates further, you can let the put option expire worthless and only lose the premium of $100,000. In this way, you can hedge your currency exposure while having limited risk and cost.

Speculating on Market Movements

Options are not just for hedging; they can also be used for

speculation. Speculation involves taking calculated risks to profit from market movements that you anticipate. Options provide a flexible and efficient way of expressing bullish or bearish views on an asset or a market.

For example, if you believe that the price of gold will rise in the next three months due to geopolitical tensions and inflation concerns, you could buy a call option on a gold futures contract with a strike price of $1,800 per ounce and an expiration date in three months for $100 per ounce.

If in three months, the price of gold rises to $2,000 per ounce, you can exercise the call option and buy the gold futures contract at the strike price of $1,800 per ounce, and then immediately sell it for $2,000 per ounce, realizing a profit of $100 per ounce minus the premium of $100 per ounce, or $0 per ounce.

Note that options can amplify gains and losses compared to the underlying asset or futures contract due to leverage and time decay. Options are powerful instruments that can be used for hedging, speculating, and generating income.

Options provide flexibility, customization, limited risk, and cheaper premiums, making them attractive for investors and traders who seek to manage their risk and enhance their returns. However, options also require a good understanding of the underlying asset, the market trends, the volatility, and the options pricing models.

Therefore, investors and traders should educate themselves on options trading before using them for their investment objectives. Nevertheless, when used properly, options can be a valuable tool in a diversified investment portfolio.

Chapter 43: Avoiding Options Trading Pitfalls

Options trading can be a highly lucrative investment strategy, allowing traders to generate significant profits with relatively small investments. However, as with any investment strategy, there are risks associated with options trading that can lead to significant losses if not managed properly. In this chapter, we will discuss some common pitfalls to avoid when trading options, as well as some strategies for managing risk and maximizing returns.

Pitfall #1: Lack of Understanding

Perhaps the most significant pitfall for options traders is a lack of understanding of the underlying principles of options trading. Options are derivatives, meaning that their value is derived from an underlying asset such as stocks, bonds, or commodities. Options contracts give the holder the right, but not the obligation, to buy or sell the underlying asset at a specific price (the strike price) within a specific time frame (the expiration date).

To succeed in options trading, it is essential to have a deep understanding of how these contracts work and the variables that affect their value, including implied volatility, the time to expiration, and the relationship between the strike price and the underlying asset's current market price. Failure to understand these principles can lead to poor investment decisions and substantial losses.

Pitfall #2: Poor Risk Management

Options trading is a highly leveraged strategy, meaning that it allows traders to control a significant amount of underlying assets with a relatively small investment. While this can lead to significant profits, it also increases the risk of significant losses, as a small change in the underlying asset's value can lead to significant changes in the options contract's value.

Therefore, proper risk management is critical when trading options. This includes setting strict stop-loss orders to limit losses, avoiding over-leveraging, and employing hedging strategies to reduce the risk of options contracts that are sensitive to market changes.

Pitfall #3: Overreliance on Technical Analysis

Many traders make the mistake of relying too heavily on technical analysis when trading options. While technical analysis can provide valuable insights into market trends, it is essential to remember that options trading is a fundamentally driven market. This means that factors such as macroeconomic indicators and geopolitical events can have a significant impact on options prices and that traders need to take these factors into account when making investment decisions.

Pitfall #4: Poor Timing

Options trading is highly time-sensitive, with contracts having an expiration date by which they must be exercised or sold. Timing is therefore critical when trading options, and traders need to be aware of market trends and have a solid understanding of the market's direction to make effective investment decisions.

For example, buying call options when the underlying asset is at its peak may lead to significant losses if the asset's value declines before the options contract's expiration date. Similarly, selling put options when the market is in a bullish trend could lead to missed opportunities for profits if the market turns bearish before the options contract expires.

Pitfall #5: Failure to Diversify

Finally, another significant pitfall for options traders is failing to diversify their portfolios effectively. Options trading can be a highly volatile market, and concentrating too heavily on a specific asset or sector can lead to significant losses if market conditions change.

Effective diversification involves spreading investments across different markets, sectors, and asset classes, including stocks, bonds, and commodities. This approach can help minimize risk and provide robust returns even in highly volatile markets.

Options trading can be a highly rewarding investment strategy, but it is essential to understand the risks and pitfalls associated with this market. By avoiding common mistakes such as poor risk management, overreliance on technical analysis, and a lack of diversification, traders can maximize their returns and minimize their risk of significant losses. By investing in a strong understanding of the underlying principles of options trading and employing proven investment strategies, options traders can achieve their financial goals and generate significant profits in this exciting market.

Chapter 44: Weekly vs. Monthly Options

Options trading can be a lucrative way to generate income, hedge against market volatility, and add flexibility to an investment portfolio. One of the key decisions traders must make is whether to buy or sell weekly or monthly options. Both types of options have their advantages and disadvantages, and understanding these differences can help traders make informed decisions about their investment strategies.

What are Options?

Options are contracts that give the holder the right, but not the obligation, to buy or sell a specific underlying asset at a predetermined price and time. This underlying asset can be anything from a stock or index to a commodity or currency. Options are sold in units of 100 shares and can be used to generate income, hedge against market volatility, or speculate on price movements.

There are two primary types of options: call options and put options. A call option gives the holder the right to buy the underlying asset at the predetermined price, while a put option gives the holder the right to sell the underlying asset at the predetermined price. Both call and put options can be bought or sold, creating a range of investment strategies to suit different market conditions.

Weekly Options

Weekly options are contracts that expire every week, typically on a Friday. These options have become increasingly popular in recent years due to their short lifespan and high trading volumes. Weekly options offer traders more opportunities for profit and can be used to hedge against unexpected market events, such as earnings releases or economic announcements.

One advantage of weekly options is their flexibility. Traders can buy or sell these options at any time during the week, allowing them to take advantage of short-term price movements. Since weekly options expire every week, traders can adjust their positions more frequently, which can be particularly useful during periods of market volatility.

Another advantage of weekly options is their low cost. Since these options have a shorter lifespan than monthly options, they tend to be less expensive. This can make them an attractive alternative for traders who want to limit their capital risk while still generating significant returns.

However, there are also some disadvantages to weekly options. One significant drawback is their limited time horizon. Since these options expire every week, traders must constantly monitor their positions and adjust their strategies accordingly. This can be time-consuming and stressful, particularly for new traders who are still learning the ropes.

Additionally, weekly options can be more volatile than monthly options. Since their lifespan is shorter, their value can fluctuate more significantly based on short-term price movements. This can create both opportunities for profit and heightened risk, depending on the trader's strategy and risk tolerance.

Monthly Options

Monthly options, also known as standard options, are contracts that expire every month, typically on the third Friday of the month. These options have a longer time horizon than weekly options, which can make them an attractive alternative for traders who are looking to invest in the long term.

One advantage of monthly options is their predictability. Since these options expire every month, traders can plan their trades in advance and adjust their strategies based on longer-term price trends. This can help reduce risk and increase the likelihood of generating consistent profits over time.

Another advantage of monthly options is their reduced volatility. Since these options have a longer lifespan than weekly options, their value tends to fluctuate less based on short-term price movements. This can be particularly useful for traders who are looking to generate steady income through options trading.

However, there are also some disadvantages to monthly options. One significant drawback is their higher cost. Since these options have a longer lifespan than weekly options, they tend to be more expensive. This can be a barrier for traders who are looking to limit their capital risk while still generating significant returns.

Additionally, monthly options can be less flexible than weekly options. Traders must hold these options for a full month, which can make it harder to adjust their positions based on short-term price movements or unexpected market events. This can be particularly challenging during periods of market volatility, where traders need to act quickly to protect their portfolios.

The decision to trade weekly or monthly options depends on a variety of factors, including the trader's investment goals, risk tolerance, and time horizon. Both types of options have their advantages and disadvantages, and understanding these differences can help traders make informed decisions about their investment strategies.

Weekly options offer more flexibility and lower costs, but they also require more active management and can be more volatile. Monthly options offer more predictability and reduced volatility, but they can be less flexible and more expensive. Ultimately, the right choice will depend on the trader's individual circumstances and investment objectives.

Chapter 45: American vs. European Options

When it comes to investing in options, there are two main types that investors can choose from: American and European options. Each comes with its own unique set of advantages and disadvantages, and understanding the differences between them is crucial in making informed investment decisions.

To begin with, American options are contracts that give investors the right to exercise their option at any time before the expiration date. This means that investors can choose to sell their option before the expiration date if they feel that the market conditions are not favorable or if they simply want to lock in their profits. European options, on the other hand, can only be exercised at the expiration date, which means that investors must hold onto their option until that time in order to exercise it.

One advantage of American options is that they offer greater flexibility to investors. Because they can be exercised at any time, investors have more control over their investment and can respond to market changes more quickly. This can be particularly useful in volatile markets, where prices can fluctuate rapidly.

On the other hand, European options offer the advantage of greater simplicity. Because they can only be exercised at the expiration date, investors don't have to worry about monitoring the market and deciding when to exercise their option. This can make investing in

European options less stressful and time-consuming.

Another important difference between American and European options is the pricing. American options generally trade at a higher price than European options, due to the added flexibility they offer. This is because investors are willing to pay more for the option to exercise their option at any time.

However, this doesn't necessarily mean that American options are always more expensive than European options. There are many factors that can influence the pricing of an option, including the strike price, the volatility of the underlying asset, and the time to expiration. In some cases, European options may actually be more expensive than American options.

One important factor to consider when investing in options is the liquidity of the market. Liquidity refers to the ease with which investors can buy and sell options on the market. Generally speaking, American options tend to be more liquid than European options, due to their greater popularity among investors.

This means that investors who are interested in buying or selling options quickly and easily may prefer American options. However, it's important to note that liquidity can vary depending on the specific market and the underlying asset being traded, so investors should do their research before making any investment decisions.

Another important factor to consider is the tax implications of investing in options. In the United States, American options are subject to short-term or long-term capital gains taxes, depending on how long the investor has held onto the option. Short-term capital gains taxes are generally higher than long-term capital gains taxes.

European options, on the other hand, may be subject to a different tax structure depending on the country where the investor is located. In some cases, European options may be subject to a value-added tax (VAT), which can significantly affect the profitability of the investment.

Overall, the choice between American and European options will depend on a number of factors, including the investor's individual risk tolerance, investment goals, and market conditions. Each type of option has its own unique advantages and disadvantages, and investors should carefully consider these factors before making any investment decisions.

Ultimately, the key to successful options investing is to do thorough research, stay up-to-date on market trends, and make informed decisions based on a combination of technical analysis and market knowledge. With the right knowledge and preparation, investors can use options to enhance their portfolio and achieve their financial goals.

Chapter 46: Options Trading Regulations and Rules

Trading in options has gained immense popularity in recent years, thanks to the flexibility it offers investors and traders in creating profitable trading strategies. Options trading allows traders to buy and sell contracts to purchase or sell assets at a pre-specified price and date. However, with great flexibility comes great responsibility, and options trading regulations are put in place to protect investors and maintain transparency in the market. In this chapter, we'll explore the regulatory framework governing options trading and the rules traders must follow to ensure compliance.

What are Options Trading Regulations?

Options trading regulations are the rules and guidelines set by regulatory bodies to govern trading in options markets. These regulations are designed to protect investors' interests by ensuring transparent and fair trading practices and providing a level playing field for all market participants.

Regulatory bodies, such as the Securities and Exchange Commission (SEC) and Financial Industry Regulatory Authority (FINRA) in the United States, play an essential role in maintaining integrity in the options market. These organizations have the power to enforce rules and initiate investigations against violators.

By complying with the regulations, investors and traders can be assured that their investments are in a safe and honest market, and any fraudulent activities are detected and addressed effectively. Let's take a look at some of the major regulations governing options trading.

Regulation T and Margin Requirements

Regulation T, also known as Reg T, is a regulation that requires investors to pay a certain amount of cash as collateral when buying securities in a margin account. The Federal Reserve Board sets the Reg T requirements, which are subject to change, and the amount varies according to the market value of the securities involved.

When it comes to options trading, an investor must have a margin account, which allows them to buy and sell securities using borrowed cash. The margin requirements for options are also set by the Federal Reserve Board, and they vary depending on several factors, such as the type of option, the underlying asset, and the time remaining until expiration.

The purpose of margin requirements is to reduce the risk of default by investors and ensure that they are financially capable of fulfilling their obligations. Margin accounts also have further restrictions on short selling shares and option contracts.

Registration and Approval of Brokers and Dealers

All brokers and dealers that trade in the options market must be registered with the SEC and receive approval from FINRA. The registration process involves providing detailed information about the firm, its managers, and the underlying assets it trades, among other things. This information is used to ensure that the broker or dealer is financially solvent and has a clean track record of trading in the options market.

Brokers and dealers must also ensure that their clients understand the risks of trading in options and that they meet the criteria for investing in such products.

Options Disclosure Documents

Investors are required to receive, read and sign the Options Disclosure Document (ODD) before taking part in options trading. The ODD is a legal document that outlines the risks of trading options and details the rules and regulations that govern trading in options markets. The document also explains the margin requirements for options trading, the process of exercising an option contract, and other critical information needed by traders.

Option Exchanges

All options trades must take place on a recognized exchange. For example, in the United States, these exchanges include the Chicago Board Options Exchange (CBOE), the New York Stock Exchange (NYSE), and NASDAQ options exchange.

Option exchanges are responsible for ensuring that all trading takes place in a transparent and fair environment. They play a critical role in establishing the rules and policies governing options trading and ensuring that all market participants follow them. Option exchanges also set the daily trading limits and have the authority to halt or postpone trading in certain circumstances.

Acquiring Options Market Data

The options market is data-intensive, and investors need to have access to accurate and timely market data to make informed trading decisions. Regulatory bodies have mandated that all market participants have access to live market data and that it is available at a reasonable cost.

Moreover, they require strict guidelines and use of trading algorithms to ensure a better pricing strategy.

Rules for Trading in Options Markets

In addition to following regulatory requirements, traders must also adhere to specific trading rules when engaging in options trading. Here are some critical rules that all traders should know:

1. Understanding their Investment Objectives

In options trading, traders must have a clear understanding of their investment objectives before placing a trade. For instance, an investor may be seeking to engage in hedging, speculation, or income generation, or some other trading strategy involving options. Each strategy comes with a different level of risk and potential return, and traders must understand the trade-offs between them.

2. Limiting Risk

Options trading is inherently risky, and traders must take measures to limit their exposure to risk. For instance, traders may implement stop-loss orders to limit their potential losses. Furthermore, traders must never invest more than they can afford to lose, as options trading involves significant leverage.

3. Monitoring Market Conditions

Market conditions can change rapidly, and traders must be prepared to react accordingly. Monitoring news and economic indicators can help traders stay ahead of markets and make informed trading decisions.

4. Buy High and Sell Low

Options trading, like other market activities, involves buying low and selling high. Traders should discipline themselves to follow this fundamental rule of trading to avoid losses.

Options trading is a popular investment strategy that offers traders flexible and versatile methods for achieving their investment objectives. However, it involves significant risks, and traders must understand and adhere to the regulatory framework and trading rules set out by regulatory bodies.

By complying with the regulations and adhering to the trading rules, traders can be assured of a transparent and fair options trading environment, allowing them to create profitable trading strategies and achieve their investment objectives.

Chapter 47: Building an Options Trading Plan

Options trading is an intriguing way to invest. When you purchase an option, you have the right, but not the obligation, to buy or sell a particular stock at a particular price before a particular date. Options can provide investors with enormous rewards, but they can also lead to substantial losses if they do not have a trading plan.

Building an options trading plan is essential for anyone considering options trading. In this chapter, we will cover the essential components of an options trading plan, including setting goals, risk management, and trade execution.

Setting Goals

The first step in building an options trading plan is setting your goals. You should ask yourself what you hope to accomplish by trading options. Are you looking to generate income, protect your portfolio, or speculate on stocks' movement?

Once you have a clear understanding of your goals, you can then create a trading plan that is tailored to meet those objectives. Some investors may choose to use options for income by selling options. Others may use options to hedge their portfolio by buying puts to protect their stocks.

No matter what your objectives are, it's crucial that you have a precise plan in place to achieve those goals.

Risk Management

Options trading can provide investors with significant rewards, but they can also lead to substantial losses. Therefore, it is essential to have a risk management plan in place.

One of the most critical components of risk management is determining how much you are willing to risk in each trade. Many traders recommend risking no more than 1-2% of your trading account per trade.

Another essential component of risk management is setting stop-loss orders. Stop-loss orders are pre-defined price points at which you will exit a trade if the stock price moves against you. This can help limit your losses in case the stock does not behave as you anticipated.

Additionally, diversification is crucial to risk management. It is best to avoid concentrating your trades in one sector or stock. When you diversify, you spread the risk across multiple stocks or sectors, lowering the risk associated with a single stock.

Trade Execution

Once you have set your goals and developed a risk management plan, it's time to execute your trades.

The first step in trading options is selecting the right one for your strategy. You can choose from either call options, which allow you to buy stocks at a pre-defined price, or put options, which give you the right to sell stocks at a set price. You can also choose between buying and selling options.

If you decide to sell options, you can generate income by collecting the premiums. However, selling options carries risks, as you may have to buy or sell the stocks if the option is exercised. In contrast, buying options can be a more straightforward way to profit since you have less risk. However, buying options also can be expensive, and if the stock doesn't move as needed, you can lose the entire premium paid.

As you execute your trades, remember to stick to your plan and avoid being swayed by emotions or impulsive decisions. One of the most common mistakes novice traders make is to let their emotions dictate their actions. By having a precise trading plan in place, you can avoid this pitfall.

In summary, building an options trading plan is essential to achieving your objectives while limiting your risk. Begin by setting your goals, then develop a robust risk management plan to protect your account balance. Finally, execute your trades with patience and discipline, sticking to your plan and strategy. When you focus on your goals with patience and discipline, you can achieve your options trading objectives.

Chapter 48: Keeping a Trading Journal

Trading can be a lucrative endeavor, but it is also risky and requires careful attention to detail and discipline. As such, many experienced traders will tell you that keeping a trading journal is a crucial part of maintaining long-term success in this field. But what exactly is a trading journal, and why is it so important? In this chapter, we'll explore the nature of trading journals, what to include in them, and how to use them effectively.

What Is a Trading Journal?

In the simplest terms, a trading journal is a record of your trades and other important information about your trading activities. It can include a wide variety of data points, from the market conditions and charts you used to make a decision to the specific entry and exit prices you used for a particular trade. By keeping track of all this information, you can gain a deeper understanding of your trading habits, strengths, and weaknesses, which can help you improve your overall performance.

Why Keep a Trading Journal?

There are several compelling reasons why traders should keep a trading journal. First and foremost, it helps you track and analyze your trades in a structured manner. Instead of relying on memory or gut feelings, you can turn to hard data to help you understand what went right and what went wrong on each trade. This allows you to identify trends over time and adjust your strategy accordingly.

Another important benefit of keeping a trading journal is that it can help you establish discipline and stick to your trading plan. By writing down your plan in advance (along with any specific rules or criteria you've set for yourself), you can refer back to it later and hold yourself accountable. This is particularly important for newer traders who may be more prone to impulsiveness or emotional decision-making.

Finally, a trading journal can be an incredibly valuable tool for those seeking to refine their strategies over time. By analyzing your past trades and identifying patterns or areas for improvement, you can develop a more targeted and effective approach to trading. This can help you to become more profitable and reduce your risk of losses.

What to Include in a Trading Journal

The specific contents of a trading journal can vary depending on your needs and preferences. Some traders prefer to keep things simple and focus on just a few key data points, while others like to include as much detail as possible. Here are some of the most common elements you might consider including in your journal:

1. Date and Time: Record the date and time of each trade, along with any relevant information about the market conditions at that time.

2. Instrument: Record the specific instrument you traded (such as a stock, currency pair, or commodity) and any pertinent details about it.

3. Entry and Exit Points: Record the specific entry and exit points you used for each trade, along with any price targets or stop losses you set.

4. Strategy: Describe the strategy you used for each trade in detail. This might include information about the indicators or other tools you used to make your decision, as well as any rules or criteria you used to determine when to enter or exit the trade.

5. Result: Record the result of each trade (profit or loss), along with any additional details about what happened.

6. Notes: Include any additional notes you want to make about the trade, such as your emotional state at the time, any lessons learned, or other observations.

7. Charts: Many traders find it helpful to include a chart with each trade, showing the entry and exit points as well as any key indicators or other data points that were relevant.

Tips for Keeping a Successful Trading Journal

While keeping a trading journal is a valuable practice in itself, there are a few tips and best practices that can help you get the most out of your journaling efforts:

1. Be consistent: It's important to make regular journal entries for each of your trades, or at least for the trades that had the most significant impact. This will help you build a solid history of your trading habits and behaviors over time.

2. Keep it organized: Many traders find it helpful to use a specific format or template for their journal entries, to ensure consistency and make it easy to read and track data. This might include using a spreadsheet, a notebook, or a specialized software tool designed specifically for trading journaling.

3. Be honest: It's important to be truthful and honest with yourself when writing your journal entries. This means acknowledging your mistakes and weaknesses, as well as your successes and strengths.

4. Analyze your data regularly: Don't just write in your trading journal and forget about it. Make a habit of reviewing past entries on a regular basis, analyzing your performance and looking for patterns or areas where you can improve.

5. Don't be afraid to experiment: While it's important to have a consistent approach to your trading journal, there's also room for experimentation and customization. Don't be afraid to try out new formats or data points to see what works best for you.

Keeping a trading journal is an essential part of being a successful trader. Whether you're just starting out or have years of experience under your belt, a trading journal can help you track your progress, analyze your trades, and improve your overall approach to trading. By being consistent, organized, honest, and analytical in your journaling efforts, you may find that you're able to achieve greater success and profitability in the markets.

Chapter 49: Continuous Learning in Options Trading

Options trading is an excellent way to earn an income. It involves buying and selling options contracts that give investors the right to purchase or sell assets at a certain price on or before a specific date. Successful options trading requires a person to have adequate knowledge, understanding, and skills. But, the truth is, the stock market is constantly changing, and what was working yesterday may not work today. Therefore, continuous learning is critical for traders to maintain a competitive edge in this market.

Why continuous learning is necessary in options trading

Options trading is a dynamic field, with a lot of information that is pertinent to making informed decisions when trading. There is always something new to learn about trade execution, risk management, and current market trends. A trader who is not committed to continuous learning risks making uninformed decisions that can result in significant losses.

Options traders must continuously educate themselves with information that could influence their trades. They must keep up with the latest news about their chosen markets, learn new strategies, and adapt to changes taking place in the market. This is important because a strategy that worked yesterday might not work tomorrow.

Moreover, continuous learning is essential in the stock market because it allows traders to avoid costly mistakes and make better decisions. With a better understanding and knowledge of the stock market, traders can avoid common pitfalls, such as making trades based on rumors, following the crowd, or failing to conduct adequate research.

As they say, knowledge is power, and the more a trader knows about the market, the better prepared they will be to make informed decisions. The continuous acquisition of new knowledge is a vital component of a trader's journey towards success in options trading.

Key aspects of continuous learning in options trading

1. Educating oneself on market conditions

The stock market is volatile, with daily fluctuations that result from unforeseen events, such as politics, the economy, and market disruptions. Therefore, a trader must identify what is driving the market and determine whether the prevailing conditions are favorable or unfavorable.

By understanding the market conditions, an options trader can adjust their strategies accordingly and take advantage of market trends. This includes analyzing fundamental indicators, such as earnings reports, news releases, and economic data to stay informed of what is happening in their market of choice.

2. Learning new trading strategies

In options trading, there are various trading strategies that traders can use to maximize their profits while minimizing their risks. Traders must make it a priority to learn new trading strategies and adapt to market changes.

One popular trading strategy that options traders use is the Iron Condor. An Iron Condor involves buying a bearish put spread and bullish call spread on the same underlying asset.

Another popular options trading strategy is the Butterfly Spread. This strategy is similar to the Iron Condor, but instead of two spreads, a trader uses three spreads to hedge their portfolio's risk.

Traders can learn about new strategies from books, podcasts, or consulting with experienced traders. However, implementing a new strategy should be done with caution, and traders should conduct adequate research before incorporating it into their trading plan.

3. Risk management

In options trading, risk management is paramount. As a trader, you must be familiar with the risks involved when trading options and how to mitigate them. This includes managing position sizes, defining risk per trade, and closing losing trades before they get out of control.

Once a trader has defined their risk parameters, they must stick to them at all times. They must also continuously evaluate their risk management strategies and make adjustments if necessary.

4. Staying up-to-date with technology

As technology continues to evolve, it is crucial for options traders to stay up-to-date with any new developments that can aid them in their trading. This includes using trading software that can make a trader's job easier.

Trading software can help with analysis, strategy development, and trade execution. A trader who is not using the latest trading software is risking being left behind in trading efficiency. As such, it is necessary to use the latest tools to stay ahead of others.

5. Accepting that occasional mistakes are inevitable

Continuous learning involves accepting that making mistakes is a natural part of the process. No one is perfect, and even successful traders make mistakes for various reasons. It is essential to embrace this and use it as an opportunity to learn and grow.

Traders must embrace their mistakes and actively evaluate what led to them, learning why they occurred and using measures to prevent them from happening again.

Options trading is a dynamic field that requires continuous learning for success. A lack of dedication to continuous learning can lead to missed opportunities, increased losses, and reduced effectiveness in trading. By maintaining a commitment to continuous learning, and implementing the skills learned, traders can stay ahead of the curve and become successful. It's essential to stay current with market conditions, inform oneself on new trading strategies, manage risk, stay up-to-date with technology, and embrace mistakes. As technology continues to evolve, the need for continuous learning and development will remain a requirement for traders to excel.

Chapter 50: Using Options Trading Software

As an options trader, you're always looking for an edge. One of the best ways to gain an advantage in the options market is by using options trading software. These tools can help you analyze trends, track your trades, and make more informed decisions when buying and selling options.

In this chapter, we'll explore the benefits of options trading software and offer tips on how to choose the right tools for your needs.

What Is Options Trading Software?

Options trading software is a suite of tools that can help options traders analyze the market, identify trends, and make better trading decisions. There are many different types of options trading software on the market, each offering unique features and benefits.

Some options trading software is designed for institutional traders who trade large volumes of options. Other options trading software is geared towards individual traders who operate on smaller scales. Some software is designed to be used on desktop computers, while others are web-based and can be accessed from any device with an internet connection.

Most options trading software is equipped with analytics tools that allow traders to analyze data and make informed decisions. These tools might include real-time charts, technical analysis indicators, and customizable dashboards.

Benefits of Using Options Trading Software

There are many benefits to using options trading software, no matter what type of trader you are. Here are some of the top advantages of using options trading software:

1. Data Analysis: Options trading software can help you analyze market data and identify trends. This can help you make informed trading decisions and increase your profits.

2. Automation: Some options trading software can automate repetitive tasks, such as placing trades or analyzing market data. This can save you time and increase your efficiency.

3. Portfolio Management: Many options trading software tools offer portfolio management features that allow traders to track their investments and analyze performance. This can help you identify areas for improvement and optimize your portfolio.

4. Access to Professional Tools: Some options trading software is equipped with professional-grade tools that are not available to individual traders. This can give you an edge over your competitors and help you make more informed trading decisions.

5. Risk Management: Options trading software can help you manage risk by providing risk analysis tools and helping you to create trading strategies that minimize risk.

How to Choose the Right Options Trading Software

With so many options trading software options on the market, it can be difficult to choose the right tool for your needs. Here are some tips to help you make an informed decision:

1. Consider Your Needs: Before you start shopping for options trading software, consider your needs and goals as a trader. Are you an institutional trader or an individual trader? Do you want web-based or desktop software? Do you need a tool that can automate trades or manage your portfolio? These questions will help you narrow down your options and find the right software for your needs.

2. Read Reviews: Once you have a list of potential options trading software tools, read reviews and testimonials from other traders. This can help you get a better sense of the software's strengths and weaknesses.

3. Evaluate User Interface: The user interface is an essential aspect of options trading software. You'll be using the software every day, so it's important to choose a tool that is easy to use and navigate. Test demos or free trials of software tools to determine which tool suits

you the most.

4. Compare Pricing: Options trading software comes at different price points. Evaluate the pricing of each software and determine whether the pricing model suits your trading style.

5. Look for Customization: Options traders have different needs, and the software should be customizable to meet those needs. Look for options trading software that allows you to customize charts, dashboards, and algorithms to suit your needs.

Options trading software can be an invaluable tool for traders looking to gain an edge in the market. By providing data analysis, automation, portfolio management, access to professional tools, and risk management features, options trading software can help you make more informed trading decisions and increase your profits. When shopping for options trading software, consider your needs, read reviews, evaluate user interface, compare pricing, and look for customization options to find the right tool for your needs.

Chapter 51: Advanced Options Strategies

Options trading offers a myriad of strategies that traders can employ, depending on their trading goals and risk appetite. In this chapter, we will explore some of the most advanced options strategies, including vertical spreads, butterfly spreads, and iron condors. These strategies require a more in-depth understanding of options trading and a higher level of risk tolerance.

Vertical Spreads

Vertical spreads are a type of options trading strategy that involves buying and selling two options of the same type (call or put) on the same underlying asset. Vertical spreads are based on the difference in the strike prices of the two options.

The two most popular types of vertical spreads are bull call spread and bear put spread. A bull call spread involves buying a call option with a lower strike price and selling a call option with a higher strike price. The opposite is true for a bear put spread, where traders sell a put option with a higher strike price and buy a put option with a lower strike price.

One of the benefits of vertical spreads is that they allow traders to position themselves for specific market trends while reducing their risk exposure. By trading two options simultaneously, traders can limit their losses and ensure that the risk is capped from the outset.

Butterfly Spreads

Butterfly spreads are a type of advanced options strategy that involves trading three options of the same type (call or put) on the same underlying asset. Butterfly spreads are based on the differences in strike prices between three options.

The three options in a butterfly spread are structured in such a way that the short option's strike price is in the middle of the long options' strike prices. This means that the short option will expire worthless, allowing traders to make a profit from the two long options.

There are two types of butterfly spreads - call butterfly spread and put butterfly spread. A call butterfly spread involves buying a call option with the lowest strike price, selling two call options with the middle strike price, and buying a call option with the highest strike price. A put butterfly spread is the opposite, with traders selling two put options with the middle strike price, and buying a put option with the lowest and highest strike prices.

Butterfly spreads are best used when a trader expects the underlying asset's price to remain stable. As a complex options trading strategy, butterfly spreads require more skill to execute, but they also offer higher potential rewards.

Iron Condors

Iron condors are a more advanced options trading strategy that involves buying and selling four options of the same type (call or put) on the same underlying asset, forming a "condor" shape. To construct an iron condor, traders will first sell one call option with a higher strike price and one put option with a lower strike price, and then buy one call option with an even higher strike price and one put option with an even lower strike price.

Iron condors are designed to generate profits in a range-bound market. Because iron condors are constructed with two offsetting credit spreads, their success depends on the underlying asset's price remaining stable over a specific period. It is essential to note that while iron condors offer higher potential rewards, they often come with a higher level of risk.

Traders who use iron condors must balance the potential risk against the potential reward and ensure they are comfortable with the strategy's risk/reward ratio.

Options trading offers numerous trading strategies, including simpler strategies like covered calls and more complex strategies like iron condors. While these advanced options trading strategies require more significant expertise and experience to execute, they also offer the potential for higher profits. However, traders should always balance the potential rewards against the potential risks before executing a trade.

Before executing any trade, traders should ensure they have a clear understanding of the underlying asset's market trends and conditions. They should also be comfortable with the risks involved in the strategy they are using. By carefully selecting the appropriate options trading strategy for their needs and risk tolerance, traders can create a successful trading plan and achieve their financial goals.

www.ingramcontent.com/pod-product-compliance
Lightning Source LLC
Chambersburg PA
CBHW051506030726
47592CB00006B/2114